Social Media Writing Lesson Plans for YouTube, Facebook, NaNoWriMo, and CreateSpace

Bonus Intro to Blogger!

ERIK BEAN, ED.D.
AND EMILY WASZAK

WESTPHALIA PRESS
An imprint of Policy Studies Organization

Also from Westphalia Press

westphaliapress.org

Rigorous Grading Using Microsoft Word AutoCorrect: Plus Google Docs

The Idea of the Digital University

Designing, Adapting, Strategizing in Online Education

France and New England Volumes 1, 2, & 3

Treasures of London

The History of Photography

L'Enfant and the Freemasons

Baronial Bedrooms

Making Trouble for Muslims

Material History and Ritual Objects

Paddle Your Own Canoe

Opportunity and Horatio Alger

Careers in the Face of Challenge

Bookplates of the Kings

Collecting American Presidential Autographs

Freemasonry in Old Buffalo

Young Freemasons?

Social Satire and the Modern Novel

The Essence of Harvard

Ivanhoe Masonic Quartettes

A Definitive Commentary on Bookplates

The Man Who Killed President Garfield

Anti-Masonry and the Murder of Morgan

Understanding Art

Homeopathy

Fishing the Florida Keys

Collecting Old Books

Masonic Secret Signs and Passwords

The Thomas Starr King Dispute

Earl Warren's Masonic Lodge

Lariats and Lassos

Mr. Garfield of Ohio

The Wisdom of Thomas Starr King

The French Foreign Legion

War in Syria

Naturism Comes to the United States

New Sources on Women and Freemasonry

Gunboat and Gun-runner

Meeting Minutes of Naval Lodge No. 4

James Martineau and Rebuilding Theology

Social Media Writing Lesson Plans for YouTube, Facebook, NaNoWriMo, and CreateSpace

Bonus Intro to Blogger!

Social Media Writing Lesson Plans for YouTube, Facebook, NaNoWriMo, and CreateSpace

Westphalia Press
An imprint of Policy Studies Organization
1527 New Hampshire Ave., NW
Washington, D.C. 20036
info@ipsonet.org

ISBN-13: 978-1-63391-159-8
ISBN-10: 1633911594

Cover design by Taillefer Long at Illuminated Stories:
illuminatedstories.com

Daniel Gutierrez-Sandoval, Executive Director
PSO and Westphalia Press

Rahima Schwenkbeck, Director of Media and Marketing
PSO and Westphalia Press

Updated material and comments on this edition
can be found at the Westphalia Press website:
westphaliapress.org

TABLE OF CONTENTS

Introduction

This book is the culmination of many months of tinkering, testing, and working with popular social media to produce viable writing lessons that can be tailored for both secondary and higher education students. And because the lessons can work equally well with higher education, we've presented the technical steps first, then the pedagogy. When we set out to design these lessons (and examine the use of sites like NaNoWriMo and CreateSpace that were already used by faculty and students alike), we knew some faculty were and are reluctant to use social media in the classroom either because their district may not allow it or they do not understand how to best incorporate it. For the most part, we've taken the guess work out and replaced it with step-by-step instructions so you can immediately set up your classroom channels. However, there is no magic panacea. Most rigorous lessons require at minimum at least an hour or two to initialize.

This volume features complete lessons for those mentioned above as well as YouTube and facebook and can dovetail our first 2014 social media lesson plan book released via Brigantine Media entitled, *WordPress for Student Writing Projects* (Bean and Waszak 2014). That book includes three lessons: A hero essay, thesis writing, and a birthday news summary and response designed to accompany a WordPress class site. Each of those assignments can be adapted to other blog sites including Google's Blogger (See Appendix F).

While no social network is 100 percent safe, teachers we collaborated with among all of our unique social media lessons report their use can help retain student attention, improve writing, and critical thinking skills (Bean and Waszak 2014). Secondary instructors can immediately benefit from the accompany rubrics that are compartmentalized for Common Core requirements. Regardless of your ties to Common Core, these lessons satisfy many other standards and can be customized for your needs.

Higher education faculty will note how easily the lessons can be tailored for traditional college semesters or accelerated ones. Most lessons are designed for blended (classes that meet both on-ground and online) environments, but with a little creativity can be adapted to 100 percent online. Finally, home school parents can work with smaller groups of students to enable these lesson plans too.

A famous Chinese proverb, "May you live in interesting times," has been both a blessing and a curse. Certainly for teachers, these are interesting times. Never before have there been so many resources to help make lesson planning easier. But with that comes choices. Another closely related Chinese proverb, "May you find what you are looking for," could be more in line with why you stumbled upon this book. As a teacher you know how important it is your lessons are rigorous while students remain attentive.

The immediacy that social networks can bring to learning is without question both a blessing and a challenge in and out of today's secondary and higher education settings. Students like most of us tend to gravitate towards things they enjoy as represented by immediacy (Mehrabian 2007). But what better place to help students experience immediacy and stay attentive than online?

Social media has penetrated our lives like no other medium and for good reason. It allows one to send and receive communications instantly to a high volume of recipients, more than any other previously developed technology. This two-way communication vehicle has numerous advantages and some disadvantages. And while every teacher's comfort level with social media varies, it is important to discuss some security and publishing risks because not all lessons using social media should be made available to the public most often only for invited classroom participants. Therefore, please be sure to consult your school's faculty handbook or faculty code of conduct before engaging in the lesson plans shown here.

Before you begin any of the lesson plans presented consider two primary risks. First, information posted should be considered permanent. Even if it is removed, backup copies may exist in computer servers from your school to Timbuktu. Secondly, it is easy to breach private information, information that could be in violation of the Family Educational Rights and Privacy Act (FERPA). We have included a generic social media student permission slip so parents have buy off (See Appendix C).

Still, in some lesson instances you will want to incorporate images to accompany the various writing practices. If you use a smartphone, for example, or other WiFi enabled digital camera, the GPS location of those photos may be stamped into the photo properties. In the following Web 2.0 Examiner.com article the location ramifications and how to remove the stamping are explained. Please see, Tech Tip Now: Unenabling the dangers of smartphone camera GPS coordinates, tinyurl.com/l896k6c (Bean2013a; 2013b; 2013c; 2013d).

With all the risks, it would seem folly to take to the social media networks to instill writing standards, Common Core or otherwise? But not utilizing the social media networks may have even more adverse student side-effects. Why? Social media is where students spend much of their free time. And while some social networks come and go, social networking is not a passing fad. It took television 13 years from 1947 to 1960 to gain an audience of 22 million. It took facebook 4 years from 2003 to 2007 to achieve that massive audience, and only took YouTube 4 months in 2005 to reach that level. Today, both facebook and YouTube have over 1 billion followers.

If students should use their own identity, using social media networks can allow your class to receive as little or as much notoriety as you deem. On the other hand, the option to create avatars for each student with a classroom key can allow anonymity as well as enabling password protected, unpublished, or non-indexed class channels, can provide more security.

Some have asked why not utilize Blackboard, Sakai, or Edmodo for such lessons? One certainly can adapt to these platforms, but even if these platforms could not duplicate all the technological features of YouTube, facebook, or Blogger, students identify and want to be part of the popular brands. Besides even if you create an unpublished YouTube class channel, for example, your students will be exposed to more video choices than any other website for sourcing, development of annotations, and to simply be part of the party, a party that teachers and students should attend (Wideen 2014).

Postman, an early technological theorist, would likely agree. He coined the term Media Ecology at the 1968 annual meeting of the National Council of Teachers of English (Strate 2004). Media ecology focuses on how society adapts and adjusted to the new role of advanced technologies. Crafting social media to instill writing standards is simply a great way to keep students engaged. Instances where other students can comment or add to the lesson make learning fun and memorable. We hope you and your students enjoy the lessons to follow and that you have a healthy approach to the latest media ecology.

—Erik Bean, Ed.D. and Emily Waszak,
February 2015

YouTube

G oogle's YouTube is the second largest Internet search engine. By creating your own YouTube class channel, you and your students will have access to the most contemporary issues, a wide variety of reputable sources and journalistic videos. Eager learners easily embrace watching videos and each can post their own videos or team vignettes based on initial in class writing assignments such as rebuttals, summaries, and poetry readings.

Developing these short videos with a simple smartphone helps to improve critical thinking, brainstorming, writing, editing, thesis defense and collaboration skills. Compared to any other available distance learning tool such as Edmodo or Blackboard, YouTube's video library, editing and privacy settings are vast, user friendly, and are accessible from many types of devices. If your school does not currently allow YouTube it may not be aware of some simple firewall coding steps that can allow a more screened version of YouTube to be enjoyed on campus youtube.com/schools (Google, 2014b).

Once accessible, your YouTube Channel can play host to many projects throughout the years. Most of these you can choose not be publically available, only a link you provide to you and your students will allow access to individual videos or a playlist, which is a YouTube feature allowing videos to be grouped based on categories or assignment projects.

Whether one has an ESL or traditional English classroom, the ability for students to comprehend information visually is seen largely in the *authenticity* of videos, authenticity that can be more readily understood (particularly globally) about any given subject than just necessarily reading about it (Mayora 2010). This authenticity does not preclude quality writing and the details that writing, reading, and listening comprehension offer.

Videos are often experienced as entertainment and thus offer another approach to capturing student attention. In the lessons to follow, your students will be writing in class via computers or iPads or tablets. They will use these writings to summarize videos or serve as scripts for rebuttals or poetry readings in videos they narrate.

Using the following lesson plans tied to your class YouTube channel can satisfy many Common Core writing standards. And the accompanying rubrics will help your students know what they did right and what they can do to improve their writing and collaborative analysis skills.

Collaborating with YouTube Videos and Comments

Scholars maintain, "We can have students evaluate what the creator's rhetorical objectives were and whether he or she met them according to the conventions of argument" (Barbeau 2010, 2). Collaborating with YouTube comments allows for freedom of speech, but there is a 500 character limit and hyperlinks are discouraged. Moderation of comments is not necessary since we recommend creating an unpublished site. Only you and your students will be posting to it. For complete YouTube community guidelines be sure to visit youtube.com/t/community_ guidelines (Google, 2014d).

Prior to 2010 YouTube had limited videos to no more than 15 minutes. While a channel owner can apply for longer ones, it is not necessary since we recommend videos less than 5 minutes. If you should choose to produce longer videos, for more information visit: <u>youtube-global.</u> <u>blogspot.com/2010/12/up-up-and-away-long-videos-for-</u> <u>more.html</u> or <u>tinyurl.com/2e7orq7</u> (Google, 2014c).

Before the First Lesson Plan

As with any social networks take some time to familiarize yourself with YouTube. Start by signing up for a new class channel here <u>youtube.com/create_channel</u> (Google, 2014a). You will be able to tie the channel to an existing Gmail or Google+ account you may have and create just about any name you wish. If you do not want the new class channel tied to an existing account, be sure to logout and then navigate to the getting started page. Even if you just have your YouTube channel web address that can suffice for now. Then continue reading below to increase your YouTube dexterity as you continue to prepare your class channel. It is a strong possibility that many of your students, particularly those in grades 9 through 12, already know the technical advice that follows.

Typical YouTube Published Page Features

Knowing the lay of the YouTube webscape will help you and your class prepare for several rewarding writing, narrating, and video analysis lessons. The typical YouTube page features the prominent displayed video in the upper left corner, the title of the video is found below it to the left, and a placeholder for an image that can be used as your English class logo as you desire. Immediately to the right is the name of the channel and the total number of videos that channel may have posted.

On the next line is the subscription button and directly to the right lies the number of subscribers. Beneath the right side of the featured video one sees the number of hits as well as likes and dislikes. YouTube differs from facebook, for example, with regard to this public voting feature since facebook opted out of using the option to dislike. These public polls are non-scientific, but allow film makers and their audiences a cursory review of public perception.

Below these features from left to right one will find the voting up and voting down icons, and starting from the middle and stretching to the right are six tabs: About, Share, Add to, Transcript icon, Statistics icon, and a report flag icon. About is preloaded with the video description below. Share allows visitors to post to any of a number of other social networks. "Add" allows one to add the video to his or her playlist, or favorites. Transcript breaks the video description down to the most prominent video script segments, but is not accurate.

Statistics show the number of video views, number of subscriptions, number of times the video might have been shared and a cumulative histogram of views since the video's inception as well as daily views. Finally the flag allows users to report inappropriate videos directly to a YouTube monitoring team. By knowing the features of YouTube you and your new YouTube class channel can be more successful.

Class Channel Access, Anonymity, and Google Identity

Since we initially encouraged you to only allow those with knowledge of your class channel to visit it, students can use pre-existing Google and Google+ accounts to post comments. Each account holder also has his or her own YouTube channel page whether he or she actively uses it or is not aware of it. But if students do not unenable their viewing history within their own channel they will be sharing the history of any video they view on your class channel.

Additionally, if students like their completed Lesson I or II video(s) to follow or another student's video, that too will compromise the unpublished address. While these actions are not likely to cause any harm, you should be aware of how YouTube keeps track of browsing.

We recommend every student take home and have signed a video agreement (See Appendix B). The purpose of the agreement is to have parents be aware of their classroom YouTube video use as well as any homework assigned related to it. In addition, the form will give you permission to establish a Google account for those that may not have one and to serve as a parental reminder of the student's existing account furnished in the letter where applicable.

Get the YouTube SmartPhone App

Via Google Play for the Android phone or via the Apple Store for the iPhone, and now the Microsoft Store for the Windows Phone, search for the base "YouTube" application by YouTube. While there are many YouTube apps that perform a variety of different functions, the basic app will allow to view your class channel when your computer is not by your side. Uploading a smartphone video will occur inside the phone's video library/gallery and/or camera software to be discussed later.

Posting and Editing Videos

Filming a simple one or two scene class video and uploading to YouTube requires little technical acumen. Various point and shoot smartphones and digital (WiFi enabled) video cameras are competitively priced and some include one touch uploads directly to YouTube. If you and your class decide to do more fancy editing we recommend software such Adobe Elements 11, adobe. com/products/premiere-elements/tech-specs.html compatible with both Windows and MAC/OS operating systems

(Adobe Systems, Incorporated, 2014). However, a novice instructor can easily shoot and post unedited videos that can readily meet the lesson demands. The time it takes depends on how many videos are uploaded concurrently and one's Internet speed. For more advanced downloading and editing of YouTube videos for incorporation in future student videos, please see Appendix A.

YouTube Beatnik
Poetry Lesson

Team Reading & Analysis
Blended: Half in-class team writing & taping /
Half individual on-line YouTube watching and collaborating

The purpose of this assignment is to strengthen creative writing and rhetoric analysis skills. A sample YouTube class channel accompanying the following lesson is located at Freshly Squeezed Student Perspectives at tinyurl.com/ku82m9n.

Historically speaking, poetry reading has existed for hundreds of years. Perhaps it was manifested on a cold evening when people gathered around a warm fire to share their passion and creativity in story telling? The exact particulars regarding the inception of poetry reading is not clear. However, poetry reading became an increasingly public phenomenon via Homer as early as 1,000 B.C. tinyurl.com/m22avno.

From Jesus Christ to the Vikings, from Shakespeare to Milton and Wordsworth, the ability to write, memorize, and recite poetry publically was a way to express love, anger, and sorrow. The Beatniks of the 1960s openly embraced poetry, a complement to folk music and a new found societal liberation. Just the thought of these melodramatic poetry sessions conjure the sounds of bongos echoing the sentiments of the poetry reader while the audience carefully pontificates and endorses the meaning of every word and phrase.

In this lesson plan your class will:

1. Divide into teams of four or five students.

2. Choose a poetry style and write a poem based on a contemporary issue that meets the poetry guidelines.

3. Recite the final poem while it is videotaped.

4. You will upload their video recital to the class YouTube channel.

5. Participate in a collaborative YouTube poetry critique comment discussion to judge the poets' creativity and whether it meets all of the required syntax style.

6. Students will be encouraged to pick out examples of figurative language and name them.

This inaugural YouTube class assignment will allow your class to flex its creativity as well as understand the particulars that make poetry writing and reading so rewarding for so many people. Many Common Core requirements as indicated in the fictional portion of Appendices Rubric will be satisfied including vocabulary, creativity, and sequencing.

Lesson Introduction (30 minutes)

Before introducing YouTube to your students, start a conversation about poetry. Ask students if they have a favorite poetry style and author. Explain that they are about to embark on a poetry exploration and no matter their level of poetry writing experience, appreciation and understanding of this popular creative writing form can prove valuable to enhancing critical thinking as well as language arts skills. Briefly celebrate the great poets, their history and success. For example, you may want to discuss Dr. Maya Angelou, visit her Website, mayaangelou.com, show a YouTube sample of a recent interview with this famous author (Angelou, 2014): youtube.com/watch?v=hSY7PokqMXk, and go back into YouTube time more than 30 years to see Dr. Angelou in her prime via the Merv Griffin Talk Show, youtube.com/watch?v=pFSjC6D5j5U (Griffin, 1982).

Perhaps your class would more readily identify with William Shakespeare, T.S. Eliot, Robert Frost, Edgar Allan Poe, or Ruth Schwartz? Visit sites like famouspoetsandpoems.com/poets.html to demonstrate the diversity of poets and the many original contributions to literature each has made throughout history (Famous Poets and Poems, 2006).

One tool to consider keeping in your poetry teaching arsenal is a Poetry Writing card deck developed by Greta Barclay Lipson, Ed.D. Originally produced for grades 4–6, we have found the cards so useful in providing simple clear poetry style definitions and requirements that also can be targeted to secondary and higher education students with little or no poetry experience. These cards clearly show more than 30 popular poetry styles and their required stanzas and syntax. Or find a resource page aboard The Academy of American Poets at poets.org/page.php/prmID/197 that also shows the requirements of the most popular forms of poetry. Here, a brief introduction is listed for a particular style. The style name, for example, Limerick, is hyperlinked to its exact syntax requirements. poets.org/viewmedia.php/prmMID/5783.

Typically, the first two lines rhyme with each other, the third and fourth rhyme together, and the fifth line either repeats the first line or rhymes with it. The limerick's anapestic rhythm is created by an accentual pattern that contains many sets of double weakly-stressed syllables. The pattern can be illustrated with dashes denoting weak syllables, and back-slashes for stresses:

1) - / - - / - - /
2) - / - - / - - /
3) - / - - /
4) - / - - /
5) - / - - / - - / -

(Academy of American Poets 2013a; 2013b, para 3).

Show a Limerick or the syntax style of another type of poem you prefer. Show a famous version of the poem style such as this limerick:

> *There once was a man from Nantucket,*
> *Who kept all of his cash in a bucket,*
> *But his daughter, named Nan,*
> *Ran away with a man,*
> *And as for the bucket, Nantucket.*

—Anonymous

Inclusion of Figurative Language

Be sure to work in a quick lesson on figurative language. Discuss the most popular types such as metaphors, simile, hyperbole, personification, denotation, connotation, Onomatopoeia, and Idioms. In fact, some of the poetry styles reflect these specific forms of figurative language. Encourage the students to work in metaphors or other figurative language they feel will make their poem engaging and memorable. We like the simple lessons offer by languagearts.mrdonn.org/figurative.html to emphasize figurative language definitions and practice worksheets. Perhaps you have another favorite lesson? The knowledge that students hold about figurative language will be put to test during the YouTube collaborative Beatnik poetry video readings.

Closing the Poetry Introduction Discussion

Close the poetry style discussion by empowering the students to believe, they too can understand, create, and produce a memorable poem, even if it does not win a Ballymaloe International Poetry Prize, considered by many to be one of the most prestigious poetry awards.

themothmagazine.com/a1-page.asp?page=10.

Ballymaloe among many such poetry contests are found throughout the Internet. Perhaps, you want to empower your class to also take part in any number of these contests? Either way, let the students know they will have support in the form of a team. Let them know that they will be co-authoring a poem of their team's choice and that the class can ultimately choose which one is best and which ones meet the required poetry style guidelines. This competitive mode will spark initial assignment interest. Some instructors like to give out prizes depending on school system rules.

Divide into Teams and Introduce the YouTube Poem Beatnik Premise (20 minutes)

We recommend teams of four students, not too small, not too large. These small teams usually elicit the best efforts from all team members. Since the poems will be written in class, you can monitor individual team participation.

1. The easiest way to divide is to examine the number of students present in class. Let's assume there is 20. Divide by 4 = 5 teams.

2. Since your goal is to have five teams of four, have each student start the count by stating his or her number sequentially up to the number 5.

3. Once the first five students know their number, repeat the process until all students know the team

they will join and have the five teams of four meet in various sections of the classroom. If you wish, you can do this step first before the initial poetry introduction discussed above.

Once the students settle into their new teams, allow them the opportunity to break the ice with one another. Good questions to ask include:

1). What is your favorite school subject?

2). Please share something unusual about yourself that no one knows. For example, that you play a particular instrument, have an unusual hobby, or a favorite food, movie, or song?

3). Have you written poems before?

4). After the mini-interview sessions are complete, each teammate is asked to stand up and to let the rest of the class know about his or her fellow peer.

Once this ice breaker is complete, ask the students to share with the class which social networks they have used. Then surprise them with the YouTube statistics shared earlier within the Most Popular Social Network overview and intersperse the history of poetry reading as discussed in the Background. Now that you have their commanding attention, explain that once the teams have carefully written their poem in class, each one will be asked to perform their poem in Beatnik style while you film their team.

It is important to note that the teams will be filmed privately so the rest of the class does not know the type of poetry style. Subsequently, during writing time, be sure to remind students not to give their work away. Inform the students that you will be posting the videos to the new class YouTube channel you previously created.

Once the videos are posted, each individual will have the ability to partake in critiquing each poem via the

YouTube commenting thread. Every student, as you will clarify, must comment on another team's specific poetry style. They will identify particular syntext as well as the poem's overall message and use of figurative language. Some instructors like to print out the collaboration rules and others may want to list the rules as a comment below each posted YouTube video. The goal is to focus on the poem's writing structure rather than the student's general opinion of the overall poem itself. You also can have each student vote for his or her favorite poem.

Optional Advanced Ethos, Pathos, and Logos, Commentary (Grades 9 through 12)

If you think your class is ready to understand the concepts of ethos, pathos, and logos, this lesson plan is a great way for students to comprehend these foundational rhetoric audience appeals. You'll find a great article about these appeals via The Chronicle of Higher Education chronicle.com/blogs/profhacker/how-to-persuade-with-ethos-pathos-or-logos/35431 or tinyurl.com/3znnbqr. Based on the definition of each, your class can analyze the poetry prose for ethos, pathos, and logos. By having students comment about specific poem lines and word choice, as related to these appeals, you help the students remove any personal bias from their critique comments.

Ethos

Ethos is the qualification of the writer and whether his or her qualifications or background come through the published piece. Obviously, one would have to really know the background of the individual, but it is important to let students know that this mode of persuasion is the most bias.

For a poem that likely has no real ill affect, but for a middle or high school essay, it would have much effect on the quality of writing. Based on the selected poetry subject, it is possible that students can decipher that the team collectively included ethos, but it will likely not be subject for analysis for this particular lesson.

Pathos

Pathos is emotion. Explain to students that when one experiences happiness, sadness, joy, insecurity, or any other emotions while reading a poem, he or she is experiencing pathos. Poets do not typically sit down and say they will be working lots of pathos into a poem, but without pathos, poems would certainly not be so appealing.

Pathos is noticeable based on the poet's word choice, the style of poem, and the sentence construction. If students are to comment about pathos in YouTube, they should not just say the poem had lots of pathos; they should point to a particular stanza, line, or word that helped elicit the emotion. By doing so you will know they have learned how to critique.

The poems should contain several instances of pathos and it may be tempting for students to critique what the poem means to them personally. Students should avoid doing this for critique purposes. Be sure to let them know it is the poem that is under the microscope, not the Beatnik performance.

Logos

Logos refers to logic, reason, and facts. If the poem contains any simple references to numbers, amounts, an argument, or premise, it is likely one could take a stance and comment that logos is present. As with pathos above, students should be reminded how to comment effectively as will be discussed.

Assigning In Class Poetry Writing

Two options exist before the poetry writing commences. Either assign one style of poem the class agrees or allow teams to pick any style. If you have a copy of the

Poetry Writing card deck discussed earlier you could divide it in quarters and pass the various poetry styles shown to each team. Allow them 10 minutes to review a style they believe they can write and one which they like.

One idea is that when competing, all the teams should write the same style of poetry. If only collaboration and critiquing are to occur, then the poetry style does not have to be the same. On the other hand, if you allow teams to choose and keep their style a secret only revealed to you, then during the YouTube critique process, you could require students to also determine the poetry style.

No matter the style, it is a good idea to set a writing time limit. One class session or 45 minutes should be appropriate. Too little time and the team cannot creatively sync. Too much time, the team may be stifled. Have teams break out a scratch piece of paper and get to work. Be sure to remind them to put their team name at the top of the paper and to write the poem in stanzas and lines as required. Let them know they can practice writing on one side of the paper and put the complete finished poem on the other.

Have them transfer the final poem via a word processor and email it to you. Lastly, instruct the students to divide the poem and have each team member memorize at least one assigned line or stanza. Or ask the team to quickly pick one to recite the entire poem while others can be encouraged to snap their fingers and/or chant. They will have some time to practice the day of the Beatnik shoot that can occur in the following class session.

Remind the students not to share their creative work with any other team. Even during the video-taping, all other teams will leave the room. Before dismissing this class session, you will furnish each student a copy of a simple one page Video agreement. See Video Agreement in Appendix B.

Preparing for the Beatnik Recording Day (60 minutes)

While you are not required to obtain a set of bongos, it is possible to include some background music as each team recites its poem. However, keep in mind that if you use pop music or any known commercial song, YouTube may flag it as a copyright violation even if your channel is not promoted nor videos publically available. On the other hand, if you only use 30 seconds of a popular instrumental it is not likely to be flagged.

Alternatively, your school's technical instructional support department may already have some type of royalty free music. Even though it is likely your school is a non-profit, copyright will prevail. Another option to spice things up is to have the other non-reading team students' chant as the other team students read the poem. Or perhaps team members can switch reading between stanzas.

After you have decided if any additional background music or sounds would be appropriate, you should consider having your students dress up for recording day. Perhaps they could wear clothing reminiscent of the turbulent 1960s, bell bottoms, tie dyed tee-shirts, and wooden high heels (if their feet may be in the video) and if they are able to obtain such clothing? Discourage clothing with logos (< brand names in this case) or sayings.

Contact the drama department to possibly schedule the shoot at your school's stage. Based on the poetry style selection it is likely the run-time for any poetry recital will be no longer 3 minutes, maybe more, maybe less. Still, it is important to have a background that is relatively free of distractions. The goal should be to make the video look like it was not filmed in a typical classroom. Classrooms tend to be too sterile.

For this lesson, consider shooting with a smartphone camera of no less than 8.0 mega pixels. Be sure the room or stage is well lit too. Try to avoid holding the camera in your hand as it will tend to shake. Instead, think about a way to prop the phone or lean it on another object if possible. One technique is to acquire a table, place the table at a point away from the stage where the entire team can be seen reading through the phone's LCD screen.

Next, stand behind the table, bend down and place the camera on the table either horizontally or vertically. By balancing phone on the table, standing behind it while carefully pinching the phone unit on the right or left side, you can keep it steady for the time you will need to record. If you have already downloaded the You-Tube app, once the filming is complete, you can easily upload it to your class site.

Video YouTube Account Agreement/Risks

To prepare for the videotaping, you'll want to have the students sign a YouTube agreement. See Appendix B. While all of your students are minors, it is a good idea to have buyoff from their parents or caregivers. Moreover, each student must have an active Google ID in order to post comments. See *Note About Class Channel Access and Google Identity* as discussed earlier.

In addition, even though you will likely opt to keep your channel only accessible to your students or parents who have its domain address, by requiring the video agreement, all stakeholders become aware of your unique lesson plan and potential risks. No last names will be mentioned in the YouTube video, but a student image is subject to duplication or misuse, although the chances are low.

Still, most parents will gladly sign knowing their son or daughter is working on an important, albeit, entertaining poetry analysis lesson. Therefore, be sure the students get a printed copy of the agreement before they go home and practice their poetry acting techniques.

The Shoot

Videoing each of the five teams should take no more than a total of 45 minutes if no out takes occur. But it is a good idea to allow teams to redo the shoot until they like it. If you have prepared as discussed above, the shoot should go smoothly. Immediately collect the signed agreements. It is a good idea to file these or scan them electronically for safe keeping later in your busy week.

It is very important the rest of the class not attend the taping. You may want to work with another teacher to keep them busy or provide something else for them to do in another arranged classroom or have them wait in the hall. Remember, the collaboration portion of the assignment is based on allowing students to analyze the poetry style and use of figurative language.

Let the students know that once all the poetry readings are posted, everyone will be expected to partake in their analysis by posting comments to YouTube. But since you have not premiered the class channel, the next time you and your students meet you'll review the critique requirements.

Uploading to YouTube (30 minutes)

Uploading to YouTube is a by-product of your smartphone's camera software and is usually initiated within the photo or video gallery where the videos are stored. Whether you have an iPhone, Android, or Windows RT based phone, the process is typically similar. For example, to initiate the upload of the first poetry reading team video, find it in your video library. Similarly to uploading to facebook, follow these steps:

1. Locate the video in your phone's video library.

2. Press and hold the video with your index finger.

3. After doing so, you should see a sub menu appear.

4. Press the new sub menu to enable the available choices.

5. In order to see YouTube, you may have to scroll down or touch See all...

6. Touch YouTube to see the available upload choices.

7. Choose a title such as "Team A: Poetry Reading"

8. Add a description that can include the first names of each team member and the date recorded. You can later add the poem from the electronic file the teams sent.

9. Security: The best selection is Unlisted. You will later then give the domain address to the students to view, but the videos will not be searchable in the YouTube search engine, nor on Google.

10. After agreeing to the YouTube rules, you can then begin the upload. This may take several minutes.

11. Repeat the process for all remaining team videos.

Alternatively, if you shot the videos via a traditional digital video camera and your footage is now on a traditional computer, then you can upload the poetry reading videos after you have logged into your class channel. Click the Upload button or drag and drop file into the "drag and drop video files" rectangular white web page space.

Fine Tuning and Personalizing the Class Channel

Consider including links to poetry style or figurative language website, ones mentioned earlier. By including relative links, your students can have more writing support materials at their disposal during the collaborative discussion to come.

If you do not plan to market your class channel for any other purposes, then you can skip these suggestions and move to Evaluations/Assessments. The channel description can include a few words about your class. But keep the description general since you may be using the channel for other writing activities as well. Once you add the description and channel navigation choices, you can toggle back and forth between the editing view and the "View as public" view. This way you can always test what the class will see. The link to toggle view can be found in the upper portion of the YouTube class web page above the main video viewing area. It is accompanied by a small global black and white icon. Finally, you can add a channel icon and art as you deem necessary.

EVALUATIONS/ASSESSMENTS

Collaboration Day

Collaboration day is always exciting particularly for one that includes videos. Congratulate the students on their team efforts. If you have a set of bongos you could invite a student to do an opening ceremony bongo roll. With the new class YouTube channel now beaming off the class LCD projector, peruse through all the creative team Beatnik poetry videos. Then start a discussion on how they will be analyzed.

Introducing Collaboration Requirements (25 minutes)

Either your class was instructed to write one particular style or you allowed them the freedom to choose any of the popular poetry styles discussed earlier. Explain to the students the following. Alternatively you could post this (edit for your class) as a comment under each team poem:

1. The first step of the student poetry analysis may include guessing the style of poetry.

2. The second or initial component is to either identify the style of poem written and recited; did the team meet the poetry style structure requirements?

3. What degree of figurative language does the poem contain?

4. What message, theme, or anecdote does the poem convey?

5. Final Option for analysis, what degree of ethos, pathos, and logos are present?

Showing and Assigning the Critique Process

Even though the poems were created in teams, individuals will be graded based on their collaboration knowledge of poetry and figurative language structure.

To help ensure each student understands how to critique and collaborate within YouTube comment fields, examine one of the Beatnik videos of your choice. If you optioned to include guessing of the poetry type, do not denote it for this demonstration.

1. Congratulate your sample Beatnik team.

2. Examine the first stanza shown in the description.

3. Focus on any noticeable figurative language.

4. Name the style of language and show the video time line in which it occurs by stopping the video at that point to defend your stance.

Show the students the hyperlinks you included to a figurative language and possibly the emotional appeal definitions of ethos, pathos, and logos. Be sure to explain that each published comment should focus on the syntax structure, not one's opinion of the poem.

YouTube Posting, Voting, Collaboration Quality (1 to several days)

Contributions to the discussion thread can physically occur anywhere on the page since YouTube features the most recent posts first. However, bear in mind that posts can be voted up and down which can affect where they are then found on the page. Encourage the students to vote for posts they deem are responsive to the requirements of poetry analysis and to vote down comments that are too trite.

No one should obviously repeat any comments made by previous students unless a student wishes to further clarify an error in a peer's analysis. Encourage students to pick at least two poems and find at least one unique figurative language syntax in each. If all of the available figurative syntax language has been commented on, students can focus on the structure of the poem, and whether such structure meets the guidelines of that poetry style.

As is the case with all such critiques, remind students that the only acceptable criticism is constructive, not destructive. By posting an occasional comment will show students that you are engaged with the collaborative nature of the lesson, particularly if you choose to have students post to YouTube as a homework assignment. Your gentle nudge such as, "Oops, you did not include figurative language in your analysis," or "Oops, I do not hear personification at that time in the video," should be enough to allow students to re-engage with the collaboration guidelines.

Initial Response and Cohort Discussion Visibility

Finally, be sure to have the students discern between an initial post and comment posts. Initial posts should be weighted more with regard to critical thinking vis-à-vis poetry analysis. Comments, those which assist other students' initial posts or those that keep the dialogue moving in the right direction should be attributed to visibility as well as poetry structure analysis. It is recommend that students respond to two Beatnik poem videos initially and provide at least four other beneficial cohort poetry analysis comments. The start and end collaboration time is up to you, but you may want to allow a minimum of two days to a maximum of one week.

Rubric Grading Reminder

We recommend you pass out the sections of the rubric to each student so they are more aptly to meet the expectations of the creative poetry writing, and collaboration lessons. Divide the rubric accordingly and to your class focus.

YOUTUBE BEATNIK POETRY LESSON

Student Name

Writing Variable	1-4 Needs Work	5-6 Fair Job	7-8 Good Job	9-10 Terrific	Score	Common Core Strand for Secondary Educators
Commenting Evidence	Did not make an appropriate effort with peers in class or electronically.	Made a minimal effort with peer support in class or electronically.	Worked well with others; demonstrated support of peers in class or electronically.	Offered extra support to those peers in need in class or electronically.		W.9-12.1 W.9-12.2 W.9-12.4-6 W.9-12.10 W.6-8.4 W.6-8.5
Comment Argument	Points are confusing and not connected to main topic.	Average development of points presented.	Evidence is presented well; needs fine tuning.	Points are valid, plentiful, clear, and concise.		W.9-12.1 W.9-12.2 W.9-12.7 W.9-12.8 W.9-12.9 W.6-8.1 W.6-8.1b W.6-8.1c W.6-8.1d W.6-8.2 W.6-8.2b W.6-8.2c W.6-8.2d W.6-8.2e W.6-8.7 W.6-8.8 W.6-8.9 W.6-8.9b
Comment Argument	Not at all convincing.	Somewhat convincing; needs more support, facts, and evidence.	Convincing, but needs fine tuning.	Excellent presentation, very convincing, strong development of argument to support comment claim.		W.9-12.1 W.9-12.2 W.6-8.1 W.6-8.1b W.6-8.1c W.6-8.1d W.6-8.2 W.6-8.2b W.6-8.2c W.6-8.2d W.6-8.2e W.6-8.9b

YouTube Beatnik Poetry Lesson

Vocabulary	Very limited range of word use; utilizes slang and/or attacks.	Some development of word variance evident; slang and/or attacks evident.	Vocabulary is at grade level; good use of variety of words and expressions.	Highly effective in using a variety of words; avoids attacks, slang, etc.	W.9-12.1 W.9-12.2 W.6-8.1 W.6-8.1a W.6-8.1c W.6-8.1d	W.6-8.1e W.6-8.2 W.6-8.2b W.6-8.2c W.6-8.2d W.6-8.2e
Poetry Creativity/ Originality	Not much effort	Decent idea, needs more creative elements such as figurative language	Includes a variety of creative elements and original ideas as figurative language	Strong effort made in making this original; creative aspects are strong as figurativelanguage	W.9-12.4 W.6-8.3 W.6-8.3a W.6-8.3b	W.6-8.3c W.6-8.3d W.6-8.3e

YouTube Controversial Issue Summary & Rebuttal

Individual Exploratory Subject, Analysis, and Defended Opinion
Blended: Half in-class writing & taping /
Half individual on-line YouTube watching and collaborating

The purpose of this assignment is to strengthen the student's perception of the connection between reading (in this case watching) and writing, and strengthen the student's ability to express opinion about the topic in text (and orally) and defend that position with supported argumentative videos. A sample unpublished YouTube class channel accompanying the following lesson is located at Freshly Squeezed Student Perspectives at tinyurl.com/lz8rjps (Bean & Waszak, 2013).

Imagine videotaping a claim or brief argument either in the form of an anecdote or third person narrative. Now imagine the equivalent of defending a claim via relative video clips rather than incorporating paraphrases and quotes. The second YouTube lesson allows students to examine a controversial issue of their choice via the largest social networking platform, summarize the controversy in narrative form including links to video clips that best defend claims made during their rebuttal.

Lesson Introduction

Students will embark on a YouTube scavenger hunt to find a controversial issue they are passionate about. They will post a written summary of the issue on the class YouTube channel accompanying their video response including links to videos that support their claims. These videos will then be combined into a You-

Tube playlist you create in order for students to have access to all of them when you provide them the unpublished link. Finally, students will collaborate amongst the playlist to assess the quality of summaries, the quality and defense of the response.

Initial Class Prep (30 minutes)

Suggested contemporary topics for grades 9–12 include: euthanasia, gun control, national debt, national healthcare, marijuana legalization, cell phones and radiation, or high unemployment. Grades 6–8 may want to examine: obesity, video game addiction, bullying, digital piracy, Apple versus Microsoft, or electric cars. Like any pursuit of background information students must find videos from reputable sources within the YouTube network. Reputable is defined by reputation—few biases, and length of existence. For example, a video found on CNN.com is said to be reputable since they are less bias (no source is 100 percent bias free) typically take a middle ground approach to delivering news, neither too far right or left, and they have been in existence for more than 30 years, a lengthy time.

Visit youtube.com/user/CNN to obtain more ideas and to guide students on contemporary issues. Be sure to scroll down to see all of the video offerings. The role of news organizations is to mirror the news, not create news. The lists of news agencies that feature videos on YouTube are many. Be sure to click the video tab to see the latest news videos of the hour. For example, youtube.com/user/ABCNews/videos features breaking news stories. The Public Broadcasting System features YouTube up to the minute news and commentary at youtube.com/user/PBSNewsHour. Certainly top notch newspapers like The New York Times are represented too, youtube.com/user/TheNewYorkTimes/videos.

Local stations and newspapers also are widely available, but may be more difficult to search for their YouTube home page. Knowing the station's call letters, corporate owner, and affiliated municipality are good Google search terms to try and locate their YouTube channel home page address link. For example, youtube.com/user/wxyztvdetroit/videos, is home to Detroit's WXYZ TV ABC affiliate and youtube.com/user/DetNewsVideo is home to The Detroit News, daily newspaper.

For profit and non-profit news agencies are bountiful within YouTube. It is important to be sure you find their home page and not extraneous videos that may have been reposted in rebuttals found on other YouTube blog channels. Blogs and individual viewpoints within YouTube can add to the lesson at hand, but typically do not come into play until students obtain rebuttal defense information from more reputable sources as discussed here.

Consider a smartphone YouTube news app such as MRRR. Search your smartphone store for YouTube news apps. This app provides quick access to the most discussed news videos; eye witnessed news videos, as well as political and natural disasters.

Of course, YouTube news related videos are not limited to strictly news agencies. Most major magazines in all segments and interests also have a YouTube channel. For example, Time Magazine, youtube.com/user/TimeMagazine, The Journal of the American Medical Association (JAMA), youtube.com/user/TheJAMAReport, and watch dog groups like the People for Ethical Treatment of Animals (PETA) youtube.com/user/officialpeta, are just some of the hundreds of high quality sources that your class can peruse through. Use these various sources as a quick lesson in source bias.

After you have set the class free to think about a controversial issue and to find a reputable videos about it, be sure students bookmark the video(s) they valued by adding the video(s) to their YouTube Channel Favorites or Watch List. The purpose of this is so they can go back to the video as many times as needed as they critically think about summarizing and responding to it.

Written Issue Summary/Video Rebuttal (one or more class sessions)

Each student will work on a one paragraph summary of the controversial issue extracted from the knowledge he or she gained from the selected video. It is a good idea to hand out the following summary guidelines and remind students they are responsible for each:

1. The lead sentence is about the topic in general. It can be a question to engage the viewer.

2. The next two to three sentences students should attribute the source of the video. For example, According to a CNN video posted on CNN's YouTube Channel on May 15, 2014 entitled, Obama Care struggles, (to follow is a one sentence summary example), CNN analyzes the latest challenges of the required healthcare program, how it affects the middle class, as well as the creation of full-time jobs.

3. Do not quote any material from the source description. Most reputable news sources will likely only have a sentence video description, not a detailed summary as required here. Paraphrasing is okay since students are paraphrasing from the video.

4. The last one or two sentences should be on why the topic is important. Students can use a simple analogy of the problem or continue to embellish on the people involved or affected.

5. Always maintain a third person voice.

6. Do not include why the student chose the topic.

7. Limit editorializing. Save all viewpoints for the response.

8. Using a combination of short and long sentences works best for sentence variety and description readability.

9. YouTube has no description limit, but it does limit the viewable description field. Viewer prospects can easily click to expand the entire description view.

10. Feel free to consult YouTube at any lesson point for more information at support.google.com/youtube/answer/57404?hl=en.

In addition, each student will work on a first or third person (voice can depend on grade level and current course objectives) response (rebuttal) that will initially be written and then read in their posted video. The summary (as detailed above) paragraph, should be written via a word processor during or after class. As discussed earlier, the summary will accompany their final posted video. The response should include the following student rebuttal:

1. Do I agree or disagree about the topic on the table?

2. Did the video source do a good job covering the topic in any selected video or a series of videos from the news source?

3. Do I have anything in common with the issue that I am willing to share with the class?

4. Or, how would I respond if I were directly affected by the situation?

5. Which two to three videos can I annotate (link to on top of the response video) to defend any possible claims I may have about the topic?

6. The response should be no shorter than 250 to 300 words and since formatting is not an issue, it can be contained in one electronic paragraph (that the student will read or memorize for their response video).

Searching for Videos to Defend a Claim (45 minutes)

Searching for videos that support the student's response will be more challenging than locating the initial reputable controversial news video(s). First the student must compose his or her response. Secondly, he or she then must focus on videos that appear reputable, but are found outside of news sources, unless they find a journalistic rebuttal of which they side. Thirdly, while you can allow a journalistic source as one of the two or three annotated sources, imbued students to search YouTube for bloggers, watch dog groups, or leaders who have more independently analyzed the controversial issue, those with a stakehold on the issue.

Finally, below this tier are other editorials, entertaining pieces, and creative works that may depict the issue as it plays out or what it might resemble over time. And while these particular videos are less reputable, they may provide a poignant defense for a student claim. Certainly such videos may not be as authoritative as a dissertation or master's thesis, but videos that can provide some statistics or further attribution of their own may provide a great argumentative defense.

Video Response Defense and YouTube Annotation Usage (One or more class sessions)

Students will link their video using YouTube's Annotation feature to those videos they believe support their claim to the controversial issue. Learn more at support.google.com/youtube/answer/92710?hl=en&ref_topic=2795929. Annotations allow hyperlinks to be embedded in the video viewing field. By doing so, students can link to other videos (they must first search for and analyze appropriately) as a defense to their controversial issue response claim. Student Jordan's video features this affect here tinyurl.com/mmfhg8e. Note how the annotation pops up over her left shoulder at about 12 seconds into her rebuttal. At 1:06 seconds a second hyperlink also appears over her left shoulder. These hyperlinks take viewers to the particular video Jordan used to defend a rebuttal claim.

We recommend having students provide 2 or 3 links to you via email so you can post these with their video summary and the video rebuttal. If you prefer not to use the annotation feature, you can include the hyperlinks by copying and pasting them with the student's video summary description, a lead into their rebuttal video. By expanding Jordan's summary, one can see the links that were duplicated there.

Reiterate to the class that the annotations will serve to defend the student's supposition, just like a paraphrase or direct quote would do so in a traditional writing assignment. While the response can be delivered in first person voice, it will be defended via authoritative sources, videos that are reputable and/or those that are directly related to the issue at hand. Students will benefit knowing that editorializing is different from defending a claim. In sum students will read their rebuttal while being videotaped. This 3 to 4 minute video in its entirety will be uploaded to the class channel in one step.

Advanced Video Editing Student Option

For more advanced technology driven students, they may download supporting YouTube videos of their choice and edit particular segments with proper video citation (Rolling credits at the end of their rebuttal) and post their complete video rebuttal package without the YouTube annotation hyperlinks. These students can use the free software mentioned earlier. They will need to download and install on their own computer or one available from your class/school. For more details on this option see Appendix A.

EVALUATIONS/ASSESSMENTS

Collaboration Day (45 minutes)

As mentioned in Lesson I contributions to the discussion thread can physically occur anywhere on the page since YouTube features the most recent posts first. However, bear in mind that posts can be voted up and down which can affect where they are then found on the page. Encourage the students to vote for posts they deem are responsive to the requirements of the summary and video rebuttal analysis and to vote down comments that are too trite.

No one should obviously repeat any comments made by previous students unless a student wishes to further clarify an error in a peer's analysis. Encourage students to pick at least two videos to analyze.

YouTube Commenting and Collaboration Quality

As is the case with all such critiques, remind students that the only acceptable criticism is constructive, not destructive. By posting an occasional comment will show students that you are engaged with the collaborative nature of the lesson, particularly if you choose to have students post to YouTube as a homework assignment.

Your gentle nudge such as, "Oops, the student's claim seems unsubstantiated, please re-examine," or "Oops, just saying great job does not meet the commenting requirements. What about the student's topic selection and hyperlinks used to defend? Did the video links appear to be quality sources?" should be enough to allow students to re-engage with the collaboration guidelines.

Initial Response and Cohort Discussion Visibility

Finally, be sure to have the students discern between an initial post and comment posts. Initial posts should be weighted more with regard to critical thinking vis-à-vis video summary and rebuttal analysis. Comments, those which assist other students' initial posts or those that keep the dialogue moving in the right direction should be attributed to visibility as well as the video summary and quality of rebuttal and defense analysis.

It is recommend that students respond to two videos initially and provide at least four other beneficial cohort analysis comments. The start and end collaboration time is up to you, but you may want to allow a minimum of two days to a maximum of one week depending on the size of your class or other concurrent required assignments. The collaboration for Lesson II is broken down as follows:

1. Student Issue Video Summary and Rebuttal
2. Initial Collaboration of Issue Summary
3. All Comments Summary Peer Feedback
4. Initial Collaboration of Response (Rebuttal)
5. All Comments Response (Rebuttal) Peer Feedback

No one should obviously repeat any comments made by previous students unless a student wishes to further clarify an error in a peer's analysis. Since the summary is published in written format under the rebuttal video, students should consider the following areas for analysis:

1. Did the student select a contemporary controversial issue?
2. Did the student effectively summarize the problem, its history, and the next steps, if any that may occur?
3. Did the student use an authoritative third person voice?

4. Did the student use proper grammar, word choice, and syntax?

5. Did the student attribute the summary to a reputable video?

Suggested Video Response (Rebuttal) Analysis

1. Was it obvious the individual pre-wrote his or her summary? (It should be. While a good narration is important, the content is more important). Have students examine the YouTube auto transcription to help make this determination.

2. Did the summary/rebuttal effectively communicate the student's opinion void of editorializing on the process? (I was asked to…or In my opinion…). These comments are not necessary.

3. If you required a third person response, did the student meet this objective?

4. Did the student use good syntax, word choice, and grammar?

5. Did the student make any claim(s) that should best be substantiated via reputable facts or statistics or history of the controversial issue?

6. Did the student include relative annotations that aptly defend a claim/supposition? Did one annotation do a better job at this than another? Were the annotations hyperlinked to reputable videos. Why are they reputable? If they are from unknown blogger (Channel Owner) was it obvious that blogger was familiar with the issue?

7. How creative was the rebuttal video? Did it go beyond the minimum of a simple camera/narrative and annotation? Did the video have any particu-

larly unique features such as lighting, background music, filters, and transitions that show the student went above and beyond the minimum assignment requirement, if allowed? If collaboration on creativity is allowed, be sure to open that portion up for comments after the initial summary and rebuttal analysis has occurred.

Rubric Grading Reminder

We recommend you pass out the sections of the rubric to each student so they are more aptly to meet the expectations of the collaborative lesson. Aside from cohort support, each category can serve as dual assessment, one for the quality of the descriptive summary and the other for the rebuttal and cohort support. Use as much or as little as you deem necessary.

YouTube Summary & Rebuttal

Student Name

Writing Variable	1-4 Needs Work	5-6 Fair Job	7-8 Good Job	9-10 Terrific	Score	Common Core Strand for Secondary Educators
Cohort Peer Comment Support	Did not make an appropriate effort with peers in class or electronically.	Made a minimal effort with peer support in class or electronically.	Worked well with others; demonstrated support of peers in class or electronically.	Offered extra support to those peers in need in class or electronically.		W.9-12.1 W.9-12.2 W.9-12.4-6 / W.9-12.10 W.6-8.4 W.6-8.5
Video as well as Collaboration Comment Evidence	Points are confusing and not connected to main topic.	Average development of points presented.	Evidence is presented well; needs fine tuning.	Points are valid, plentiful, clear, and concise.		W.9-12.1 W.9-12.2 W.9-12.7 W.9-12.8 W.9-12.9 W.6-8.1 W.6-8.1b W.6-8.1c W.6-8.1d / W.6-8.2 W.6-8.2b W.6-8.2c W.6-8.2d W.6-8.2e W.6-8.7 W.6-8.8 W.6-8.9 W.6-8.9b
Rebuttal Argument	Not at all convincing.	Somewhat convincing; needs more support, facts, and evidence.	Convincing, but needs fine tuning.	Excellent presentation, very convincing, strong development of argument to support comment claim.		W.9-12.1 W.9-12.2 W.6-8.1 W.6-8.1b W.6-8.1c W.6-8.1d / W.6-8.2 W.6-8.2b W.6-8.2c W.6-8.2d W.6-8.2e W.6-8.9b

YouTube Summary & Rebuttal

Vocabulary	Very limited range of word use; utilizes slang and/or attacks.	Some development of word variance evident; slang and/or attacks evident.	Vocabulary is at grade level; good use of variety of words and expressions.	Highly effective in using a variety of words; avoids attacks, slang, etc.	W.9-12.1 W.9-12.2 W.6-8.1 W.6-8.1a W.6-8.1c W.6-8.1d	W.6-8.1e W.6-8.2 W.6-8.2b W.6-8.2c W.6-8.2d W.6-8.2e
Grammar	There are 15 or more serious grammar errors.	There are fewer than 15 serious grammar errors	There are fewer than 10 serious grammar errors	There are no serious grammar errors	W.9-12.4 W.6-8.3 W.6-8.3a W.6-8.3b	W.6-8.3c W.6-8.3d W.6-8.3e
Mechanics/ Spelling	There are 15 or more errors in spelling, capitalization, punctuation, and end marks.	There are fewer than 15 errors in spelling, capitalization, punctuation, and end marks.	There are fewer than 10 errors in spelling, capitalization, punctuation, and end marks.	All sentences use correct spelling, capitalization, punctuation, and end marks.	W.9-12.1 W.9-12.2 W.6-8.1 W.6-8.1c W.6-8.1d	W.6-8.2 W.6-8.2c W.6-8.2d W.6-8.2e
Video Summary	Summary not clear and concise; introduces new information; does not reiterate thesis.	Summary in development stage; needs work.	Decent summary, but could be stronger.	Summarizes, does not introduce new information, reiterates thesis.	W.9-12.1 W.9-12.2 W.6-8.1 W.6-8.1c W.6-8.1d	W.6-8.1e W.6-8.2 W.6-8.2d W.6-8.2e W.6-8.2f

YouTube Middle School
Adaptation Example

In this unpublished example, tinyurl.com/p7mufvg North Kansas City Public Schools 7th Grade English Language Arts Teacher Karen Salsbury demonstrates a twist to the summary and rebuttal lesson. Karen is the webmaster of a popular and award winning teacher's lesson plan site dubbed, Teacher1stop.com. The site recently released two complete teacher lesson plans, *Argumentative Essay Instructional Curriculum: Incorporating Companion English Language Arts Standards Simultaneously*, November 2013, and an *Informational Text version*, April 2014. The next book due in Fall 2014 is entitled Writing a Narrative Instruction Curriculum.

She adroitly understands the mindset of learners this age. In her adaptation, 10 students showcase their views in a slideshow format. Shy students are not seen, but definitely have a voice and "By not showing students, privacy becomes a non-issue for public schools and parents," Karen said.

From an iPad and Microsoft Surface comparison to how a nickel metal hydride (NiMH) battery works and commentary on bullying to obesity, Karen's students demonstrated a high level of subject matter absorption and expression. However, did they collaborate rigorously? Karen said, "The collaborative piece was not used since the assignment began later in the semester. However, this initial adaptation, the focus was on choosing a subject via quality YouTube available videos and having the students summarized what they learned. The students superseded this assignment step when time ran out."

She agreed the implementation was a great learning process and her students were so eager to prepare their slideshow videos. Another important lesson was just using the technology in the classroom particularly since her students had received iPads for this purpose. "Next year I plan to incorporate the collaborative piece as springboard from this experience," she said.

YouTube & Facebook Quality Video Source Analysis

Individual Viewing & Analysis
100 percent online facebook collaboration of YouTube video source quality

Overview

In this lesson that utilizes critical thinking skills such as: interpretation, analysis, evaluation, inference, explanation, and self-regulation, students will examine a reputable YouTube video from the list of reliable sources discussed in Lesson II, and then deliberate the relationship between causes and effects.

You can post your call for a cause and effect conversation under the YouTube "Discussion" tab. However, you can only hyperlink to the video, it cannot be embedded. Students who in a previous lesson had access to commenting, can continue to do so under this Discussion tab. Do be mindful of posting here since the default also will post the comment to Google+. However, the privacy can be controlled based on your Google+ circles, customers, or those that follow you in Google+. Additionally, you can enable the posting to be private so that like in previous lessons, only those with a link or who subscribe to the page can view it.

Alternatively, if you do not like the tie in to Google+ or the inability to embed video in your YouTube class channel Discussion page, you may want to hold the discussion in a facebook class group. A Facebook group can be used for a variety of other future class projects. If you wish to hold the discussion in YouTube, skip to Collaboration Overview. If you wish to hold the discussion in Facebook, continue below to Setting Up a Facebook Group.

Setting Up a Facebook Group (45 minutes)

In facebook, you can embed the video so students can watch it there, and rigorously comment on it, as you keep a careful watch of the unfolding discussion. In addition, you can use your facebook group page for new future lesson plans. You will begin the discussion by asking students to deduce the video main ideas.

Subjects such as fast food consumption, too much social networking, or lack of exercise are great topics to start. As students comment in facebook their postings will not be visible to their own facebook history so they can feel comfortable to freely express themselves. Students as well as you can like the comments that add value to the conversation and meet posting guidelines to be discussed later.

Start a new class group managed off your existing facebook page. The first step in this process is to choose a name for the group and facebook will immediately tell you if the name is available. Do the following:

1. While on your personal facebook home page, look for the label "Groups."
2. Scroll down to "Create Group," and select.
3. A new smaller browser window will appear allowing you to choose a group name. Be strategic and select a name that is reflective of your classroom goals, one that you and students can be proud.
4. You must invite one friend, preferably a student who is a current friend to initiate the group, otherwise the group cannot be formed.
5. Select Closed group then click "Create."
6. Once the group is formed visit the "Settings" icon. This looks like a tiny gray gear on the right hand side of the upper tab menu bar.

7. Once in Settings you can solidify a permanent email address as well as web address to provide your students, if desired. Any name longer than five characters if available can be used.

8. You may want to align the web address and email address with the group name, but facebook does not do this automatically. You also can select a miniature icon to represent the group such as a green apple.

9. You can write a group description of your choice.

It is important that you establish a group rather than a standard standalone page. Groups allow you to include friends and student invites who will see posts, but the public will only see that the page exists or you can choose to keep the group secret so that only students invited can see it. When you start to manage your facebook group, we also recommend not to moderate posts. In other words, do not hold posts for approval. The immediacy of seeing the cause and effect discussion unfold is paramount to student creativity and attentiveness.

Collaboration Overview

The success of collaborations in the classroom and online is attributed to rigorous analysis and comments. To achieve this, post the collaboration requirements in your YouTube discussion thread or Facebook group. In YouTube post the suggestions to follow as simple discussion text or consider posting a slide show recording or short video you develop that highlights the important collaborative rules. In Facebook the process can begin with a Status update or the group allows for attachments. You could post a PDF file with the rules tailored for your class and grade level.

Class Assignment Introduction (45 minutes)

Initiate a class discussion on the concept of cause and effect. Gathering reliable background information is the first step. For example, you may want to discuss vehicle exhaust and greenhouse gases and examine a government website like tinyurl.com/n35mxr2. or the relationship between plants use of carbon dioxide and their contribution to oxygen and include in the discussion an educational website such as: water.me.vccs.edu. Explain why these sources are generally reliable because one is from a government report and the other a lesson from a school.

These sources would generally be regarded as quality background information or thesis defense material for most any essay or claim due to their reputation and few biases present. However, both of these controversial issues bring with them varying opinions on whether or not the environment is drastically affected, whether mankind has substantively contributed to their danger levels, or whether nature goes through a natural progression or cycles of pollution caused by weather, solar flares, and by products of all living matter. Now ask students to consider how to locate a valid source in YouTube based on reputation and as described in Lesson II?

Searching and Posting Reliable Background/ Source YouTube Videos (45 minutes)

Should you choose greenhouse gases as your YouTube cause and effect collaboration you could select such a video from any number of reputable YouTube channels. For example, this approximately 3:30 minute one posted in 2012 from NASAEarthObservatory brings with it the National Aeronautics and Space Administration reputation on atmosphere science. youtube.com/watch?v=ZzCA60WnoMk.

1. Searching Google for this reliable source took less than 5 minutes using simple terms like, "YouTube, greenhouse effect." You can try adding a reputable journalistic or organization name, but it may not necessarily increase your retrieval success if you were not aware of many corporate, government, and scientific divisions and agencies. You will retrieve more videos by keeping the terms simple.

2. Study who posted the video which will clearly include the date and the words "Uploaded by..." Here a video was uploaded by NASAEarthObervatory. One can feel confident that the video comes from the government agency division.

3. By clicking on their name, indeed the viewer is taken to the NASA division YouTube home channel.

4. Searching for such reliable videos also can be accomplished through YouTube itself but not necessarily faster or with better results. If you search inside YouTube you need not include "YouTube" as a search term.

5. Finally, post a link in your class YouTube channel discussion tab with a prompt such as, "Let's discuss the causes and effects of Global Warming as outlined in the following NASA video." Likewise, if

using Facebook the video can easily be embedded by copying the URL into your class group page (Using YouTube embed code is not needed).

6. The same in class discussion can occur online.

Searching for Opposing Views

As mentioned earlier varying opinions on how the controversial issue affects the environment are many. Now engage the class on opinions and what shapes them and what biases can affect them.

EVALUATIONS/ASSESSMENTS

Collaboration Day (One or More Class Sessions)

Similar to previous YouTube lessons in this book, no one should obviously repeat any comments made by previous students unless a student wishes to further clarify an error in a peer's analysis. Encourage students to pick at least two videos to analyze.

YouTube Commenting and Collaboration Quality

As is the case with all such critiques, remind students that the only acceptable criticism is constructive, not destructive. By posting an occasional comment will show students that you are engaged with the collaborative nature of the lesson. Remind students how to judge the quality of any source, let alone a video. Print has been the mainstay for centuries, but video will continue to grow and its influence on issues, how reputable it is, and the nature of the organization that publishes it, must all be considered.

Initial Response and Cohort Discussion Visibility

Finally, be sure to have the students discern between an initial post regarding their interpretation of the video source quality opposed to commenting on their peers. Initial posts should be weighted more with regard to critical thinking as noted earlier. Comments, those which assist other students' initial posts or those that keep the dialogue moving in the right direction should be attributed to visibility as well as the video summary and quality of rebuttal and defense analysis.

The start and end collaboration time is up to you, but you may want to allow a minimum of two days to a maximum of one week depending on the size of your class or other concurrent required assignments.

1. Initial Collaboration Quality

2. Peer Constructive Feedback

Adapt the following rubric for your class needs:

YouTube & Facebook Quality Video Source Analysis

Student Name

Writing Variable	1-4 Needs Work	5-6 Fair Job	7-8 Good Job	9-10 Terrific	Score	Common Core Strand for Secondary Educators	
Cohort Peer Comment Support	Did not make an appropriate effort with peers in class or electronically.	Made a minimal effort with peer support in class or electronically.	Worked well with others; demonstrated support of peers in class or electronically.	Offered extra support to those peers in need in class or electronically.		W.9-12.1 W.9-12.2 W.9-12.4-6	W.9-12.10 W.6-8.4 W.6-8.5
Video Source Initial Collaboration Comment Evidence	Points are confusing and not connected to main topic.	Average development of points presented.	Evidence is presented well; needs fine tuning.	Points are valid, plentiful, clear, and concise.		W.9-12.1 W.9-12.2 W.9-12.7 W.9-12.8 W.9-12.9 W.6-8.1 W.6-8.1b W.6-8.1c W.6-8.1d	W.6-8.2 W.6-8.2b W.6-8.2c W.6-8.2d W.6-8.2e W.6-8.7 W.6-8.8 W.6-8.9 W.6-8.9b
Vocabulary	Very limited range of word use; utilizes slang and/or attacks.	Some development of word variance evident; slang and/or attacks evident.	Vocabulary is at grade level; good use of variety of words and expressions.	Highly effective in using a variety of words; avoids attacks, slang, etc.		W.9-12.1 W.9-12.2 W.6-8.1 W.6-8.1a W.6-8.1c W.6-8.1d	W.6-8.1e W.6-8.2 W.6-8.2b W.6-8.2c W.6-8.2d W.6-8.2e

YouTube & Facebook Quality Video Source Analysis				
Grammar	There are 15 or more serious grammar errors.	There are fewer than 15 serious grammar errors	There are fewer than 10 serious grammar errors	There are no serious grammar errors	W.9-12.1 W.9-12.2 W.6-8.1 W.6-8.1a W.6-8.1c W.6-8.1d	W.6-8.1e W.6-8.2 W.6-8.2b W.6-8.2c W.6-8.2d W.6-8.2e
Mechanics/ Spelling	There are 15 or more errors in spelling, capitalization, punctuation, and end marks.	There are fewer than 15 errors in spelling, capitalization, punctuation, and end marks.	There are fewer than 10 errors in spelling, capitalization, punctuation, and end marks.	All sentences use correct spelling, capitalization, punctuation, and end marks.	W.9-12.1 W.9-12.2 W.6-8.1 W.6-8.1c W.6-8.1d	W.6-8.2 W.6-8.2c W.6-8.2d W.6-8.2e

Facebook Class Fictional Writing Caper

We suspect the one social network that needs the least introduction is facebook. Note that we do not capitalize the name to stay true to its brand. With more than one billion subscribers, facebook is to social networks what Ford was to the automobile, what Edison was to electricity, and is what Tesla is to the electric car. More students will likely have access to facebook than any of the other social networks we've discussed. That means students also can likely navigate through facebook more readily and may stand poised to effectively contribute, since many of them already spend time here.

While rumors persist that facebook may have peaked, it continues to offer an easy way for families to stay in touch, even if some children are migrating to separate themselves from the old generation. When combined with smartphone app accessibility, facebook has become a repository of individual and family story chronicle events, and consumer and political endorsements, the likes of which have never been available on any single website.

What can facebook do?

1. The site allows for status updates (free verse thoughts that users share publically, with friends of friends, just friends, or privately to a custom set of friends), this can include one's location if he or she chooses to reveal.

2. Anything shared publically will be picked up by Google's search engine. And while the lessons below will appear in private facebook groups, it is important to be aware of security that could lead to unwanted facebook traffic.

3. Allows for asynchronous discussion (participants can contribute to the changing dialogue anytime) of synchronous discussion (participants can see the conversation unfold in the news space or have private chats with one another).

4. Additionally, one can upload photos and videos, as well as like and subscribe to other facebook pages, those of corporate, non-profit, watchdogs, religious, or hobby pages. Uploading student photos and allowed students to like particular story passages are important to the collaborative nature of the lessons.

5. facebook offers a variety of online games to compete with others for points, public praise, and contest awards. These amenities are not included in the lesson plans, however.

6. Creating a class group will allow you to post files such as Word documents and PDF files. These will come in handy for a variety of lessons.

7. Students age 13 and above can freely sign up for a page and post inside your class group page with confidence since your group will not be publically viewable.

The behemoth or omnipresent social networking site opted out of a dislike option (available in YouTube) probably due to unwanted advertising negativity. Once a user likes a facebook page he or she then receives updates that are posted via his or her newsfeed page. Based on security settings one can post a note on another user's home page also known as his or her wall.

Finally, one can expand his or her network by inviting other "friends" to connect. Note that according to facebook's user agreement, all material posted becomes the property of facebook, including photos and videos, for example. If facebook wishes to use these materials for advertising or offer them for sale in any format, it may do so. However, thus far facebook has mostly capitalized on user likes. When likes are combined with paid advertising, users effectively endorse a product and such an endorsement can make its way to millions of facebook subscribers.

The lesson to follow will flourish around a new facebook class page, one where students must subscribe and where the contributions made will not be publically available unless you and your students agree. Based on the end writing and collaborative product, you may choose to publish your students' work in a compendium via CreateSpace.com, for example. The virtual sky is the limit. You may consider publishing and making the work available for sale and later donate the revenue to a class cause.

Creative writing takes on a new twist in this facebook caper your class will collaborate on including character development and dialogue as well as uploading pictures of key settings coupled with their chosen classmate protagonist, antagonist, round and flat characters. During the progression of the story and after it concludes you can download a free PDF of the facebook tale to assess the quality of student contributions via the accompanying appended rubrics and as a student keepsake for years to come. You will know exactly who contributed each piece of the story as well as the number of classroom likes particular passages and dialogue garnered. This assignment reinforces fictional storytelling, sentence construction, dialogue, sequencing, plot, and closure. Some pre-facebook story criteria will be necessary in class before the story can unfold online.

Before the First Lesson Plan (Time—20 minutes)

As with all the social networks discussed in this series, take some time to familiarize yourself with facebook, particularly if you do not have an account. You will want to start a new class group managed off your existing facebook page. The first step in this process is to choose a name for the group and facebook will immediately tell you if the name is available. Do the following:

1. While on your personal facebook home page, look for the label "Groups."

2. Scroll down to "Create Group," and select.

3. A new smaller browser window will appear allowing you to choose a group name. Be strategic and select a name that is reflective of your classroom goals, one that you and students can be proud.

4. You must invite one friend, preferably a student who is a current friend to initiate the group, otherwise the group cannot be formed.

5. Select Closed group then click "Create."

6. Once the group is formed visit the "Settings" icon. This looks like a tiny gray gear on the right hand side of the upper tab menu bar.

7. Once in Settings you can solidify a permanent email address as well as web address to provide your students, if desired. Any name longer than five characters if available can be used.

8. You may want to align the web address and email address with the group name, but facebook does not do this automatically. You also can select a miniature icon to represent the group such as a green apple.

9. You can write a group description of your choice.

It is important that you establish a group rather than a standard standalone page. Groups allow you to include friends who will see posts, but the public will only see that the page exists or you can choose to keep the group secret so that only friends invited can see it. When you start to manage your facebook group, we also recommend not to moderate posts. In other words, do not hold posts for approval. The immediacy of seeing the story unfold is paramount to student creativity and attentiveness.

Convert Your Completed Facebook Page to a PDF (30 minutes)

This technique is optional at the end of the lesson, but can add value as a keepsake long after your class facebook group disassembles or before you choose to delete posts making way for your next class iteration. Imagine if anyone you deem necessary, for business or pleasure, could take your facebook site and easily print it out, use it as a wall poster, flyer, or handout?

Having a PDF of your class facebook site will allow you to attach it to student emails. You can forever cherish those creative story contributions long after the last day of class and provide a complete story to parents as well. Having a PDF handy can prove valuable as a great assessment tool, particularly since the creative writing assignment will satisfy many Common Core standards shown in the accompanying rubrics.

There are several tools throughout the Internet available to take your class facebook group or personal facebook site and convert each to a PDF. If you are technically savvy, you can do this at no cost by following the steps via this link tinyurl.com/auocpht. However, this process can be lengthy.

If you are not technically savvy or you simply do not have time, several sites including mysocialbook.com will automatically convert your class facebook site to a PDF for as little as $19.95. You will have to share your facebook contacts with the service as well as like and post your action to your network. Once you do, MySocialBook.com will send your PDF to your personal email.

The conversion to PDF typically takes the most popular pictures, videos, discussions, and likes for PDF assembly. However, since your facebook class group is new compared to facebook sites with several years of posts, the PDF conversation should end up grabbing most every student contribution. The PDF also includes any posted hyperlinks. The service even allows you to choose a specific background page color to help make your class group stand tall should you decide to use it as a class poster. This service also offers complete facebook hardcover books and photo albums.

Story Parameter Preparation (45 minutes)

Selecting the Genre

Start the preparation by first selecting the story genre your class is most interested. Choose from the following: mystery, western, action, romance, or science fiction. We recommend staying away from pure comedy. Consider working in a discussion on setting and perhaps consulting any number of books on the topic. When students begin their story telling in facebook, they should have a good feel for establishing a believable fictional setting that should draw from relevant setting artifacts pertaining to a particular era. Books such as: The Writer's Guide to Everyday Life in the Wild West: 1840 to 1900 (Writer's Guides to Everyday Life), tinyurl.com/kg7omh8, The Writer's Guide to Everyday Life in the 1800s (Writer's Guides to Everyday Life), tinyurl.com/qcf78gu, The Writer's Guide to Everyday Life from Prohibition Through World War II (Writer's Guides to Everyday Life), tinyurl.com/o3vjqya, Description & Setting: Techniques and Exercises for Crafting a Believable World of People, Places, and Events (Write Great Fiction), tinyurl.com/nfu2byx, can be excellent resources for demonstrating the need to develop a successful setting.

Character Brainstorming (45 minutes)

Brainstorming, as you will explain to the class is the initial story building process. Continue the lesson with a discussion on the definitions of the protagonist, antagonist, flat, and round characters. You may want to examine any number of websites for quick definitions such as learn. lexiconic.net/characters.htm. Then select class members who will represent the protagonist and antagonist.

Bear in mind that the selection does not refine these student roles to the writing necessary to develop the characters. Their likeness will simply represent the role in pictures posted to your facebook class group albums. The use of selected student characters helps build story development interest. Students like seeing themselves and classmates online. Set aside some time to take their photos in class with your smartphone camera. Be sure to disable to GPS setting within the camera options so the location will not be available in the photo properties even though your group will remain closed.

Create a new album for each category of character. Everyone should have his or her photo taken to feel completely connected to this story-building lesson. Later in our lesson plan, we will discuss how student facebook like votes can sway the direction of the story as it unfolds. In the event of a tie where text dramatically affects the story outcome of the protagonist, antagonist, or round characters, the class will vote to determine the story destination.

Assigning Student Characters (30 minutes)

You could select a number of methods to assign the characters. The hat or fish bowl method usually works well. On little pieces of papers, write up one for the protagonist, one for the antagonist, six for the round characters, 10 for the flat characters, and 7 for narrators. Have each student make a selection. Then build a list of their assigned roles. When students start contributing to the Almost Never Ending Story via the facebook comment features they must first decide what role their contributing text represents? Are they posting as the protagonist, antagonist, round, or flat character? On the other hand, are they posting as the narrator to provide more story setting description and or character background information?

Revealing the Class facebook Group (20 minutes)

Now that you have set up your class facebook group, determined the story genre, discussed the setting, and assigned the student characters, you can reveal your facebook group on your classroom computer via an LCD projector. Assuming students are currently active on facebook, invite them to officially become a group member. Either students must have been a facebook friend or you can invite them via an email address each must furnish. Once logged into your facebook class group, the invite feature is found in the right column. Perhaps your school has an email account for each student? Enter the addresses and remind them to accept your invitation either immediately in class if they have computer, iPad, or tablet access or that evening at home. Alternatively, you can send a piece of paper around to obtain their email addresses.

Assigning facebook Story Posts and Ground Rules (30 minutes)

Assigning the number of student facebook posts and rules governing the creative freedom that are the basis of the lesson is a necessity. Use these recommended guidelines or make up your own:

1. Students can post as the narrator or any single character they wish on a daily basis, but no fewer than two posts and no more than three per day allowed. Students should take time to comprehend the current story direction. They should critically consider how their prospective creative post would affect the setting and/or plot. Therefore, they should carefully think before they post.

2. On a weekly basis, students must contribute one of all possible story roles: narrator, protagonist, antagonist, round, or flat character. They should be prepared to discuss the quality of their contributions in class during a weekly class story roundup.

3. If contributing dialogue, direct quotes must surround all spoken words accompanied by a past tense verb or adverb, and clearly include the individual character speaking. For example, "This town is not big enough for the both us," Jordon said seriously. < The order is up to the writer. For example, in a serious voice Jordon said, "This town is not big enough for the both us."

4. Story Influencer: Every student has a chance to not only influence the story via his or her post, but to vote on which posts make the characters and setting more believable or the plot more meaningful. In order for the voting to be meaningful and to avoid over voting clutter within the comments, students should be allowed to vote a maximum of three votes per day. Votes are used by students and by you as the publisher as a tool guiding the direction of the story. Bear in mind that many posts will contain no votes. Since facebook does not use a thumbs down option, these absentee votes will need your publisher's eye to keep or delete.

5. <u>The instructor</u> reserves the right to remove any post at any time by simply clicking the hidden "x" in the upper right corner of the post itself. However, if you choose to do so be prepared to tell the class why in a publisher's post as close to the offending post. Reasons for removing posts may include poor grammar, outrageous statements that do not follow logically, or story redundancies. Note that the comment feature in facebook is flat, meaning no indentation is possible for dialogue or your directional posts. Your posts indicates only one purpose, you are providing story direction or feedback on story contributions.

6. Briefly explain that their grade will be based on quality story contributions and that once posted students should not later remove them.

EVALUATIONS/ASSESSMENTS

We suggest you use any and all parts of the accompanying fictional rubric located in Appendix D. Use the Likebook PDF as a tool to easily see how posted. You could print and distribute one to each student coupled with the sections of the rubric you feel work best. Consider taking the final story and having that published in any number of other formats and if you feel the story is truly excellent considering offering it for sale through CreateSpace. Split the profits with all class members or donate them to a charity.

NaNoWriMo:
A November Novel Lesson

Writing assignments can often bring a feeling of dread for the student, but imagine instead of simply assigning a project, you extend a challenge to the student. Imagine setting a foundation in which a student is only able to succeed by offering the student the chance to develop an assignment, an assignment based on an outline you provide specifically customized for each student. When you offer the student the opportunity to customize his or her own assignment to his or her own abilities, desires, and goals, the end product should offer much more visible effort and passion presented by the student.

November is an ideal month to work on narrative writing using social media because of NaNoWriMo.org National Novel Writing Month. The premise is that an individual uses that month to write a novel beginning to end. This project began in 1999, and the goal has always been to write 50,000 words in 30 days; this is the "adult" version. In its first year, there were 21 participants and six winners. By 2011, it had grown to 256,618 participants and 36,843 winners. In 2005, there was the addition of the Young Writers Program, and over 100 K-12 schools participated. In 2011, that number reached 2,000, according to NaNoWriMo! This has been well-utilized in the schools, and it only continues to grow. In addition, several authors have found publishers, including New York Times #1 Bestseller "Water for Elephants" by Sara Gruen. While this is not common to find this sort of success, imagine the motivation this gives to your students!

It is a challenge, a goal, a mission. Beware: it may become a bit competitive in the classroom setting, and it will become what could be the most fun assignment of the year! Completing an already-begun project is not allowed. The site allows the writer to track his/her progress, receive pep talks, and meet other writers. You may be wondering how in the world your students will write 50,000 words in 30 days. That is a huge undertaking for an adult.

Here is the great news: NaNoWriMo offers a Young Writers Program for use by educators designed specifically for kids and teens. Participants ages 17 and under set individual word-count goals, and support is offered through an engaging, youth-oriented site which offers plenty of noveling (What UrbanDictionary.com defines as "A long or overly wordy text message or social network update, 2013, para 1") resources. But for students and teachers alike, each has the opportunity to write a traditional novel. It also provides free educator resources—including curricula, workbooks, and a classroom kit—for teaching NaMoWriMo in schools, libraries, and community centers. Educators are able to easily obtain these materials well in advance to review and plan for this intense project.

Upon completion of the program, participants and educators report positive results in writers' self-confidence, creative writing skills, overall writing skills, and time management. This also is a project in which the educator may be an active participant and complete a novel, as well. What a fabulous opportunity to engage with the students and live the experience together!

This site allows each student to customize the assignment to what best suits him/her. With your assistance, your student will determine the word goal for the month. While you could set a "class" goal, it is imperative to "customize," especially for students with learning disabilities, in order to generate a positive writing environment and avoid frustration for the student. The student will then need to develop a plan for proper time management to accomplish this goal.

The goal should be challenging yet attainable in order to allow the student to complete the assignment while developing creative writing skills. It should be noted that the development of the novel is critical in this month. The focus should not be on editing as one writes, but instead, a focus on the free-flowing thoughts, plot and character development, and the story line should be the goal in the first 30 days. There will be plenty of time for self-correction and revisions following the month of writing. This is the month dedicated to creativity!

While it would be easier on the educator to utilize the offerings of the NaNoWriMo site in November, it is possible to tailor this to another month to better serve your schedule. You may opt to create your own blog, possibly by setting up a private page on Facebook, for students to communicate and update their own word counts. You would then customize with each student his or her particular plan, as noted above. It would behoove you to participate in the November event, even if you do not complete a novel, to get a feel for how the program runs and customize your own lesson plan accordingly.

Guidelines for the assignment are clear-cut: the student must create a novel based on his or her interest while focusing on plot development, character development, time sequence, and the use of proper grammar and sentence structure. The student will develop strength is developing narrative text. This assignment meets several of the common core standards.

This assignment will take minimal classroom time, and it does not require Internet, computer, or iPad access within the school. Ideally, this assignment is meant to supplement coursework and is to be completed at home via use of the Internet. The goals should be set with the clear understanding that they may be met with an hour or less of homework per evening. Classroom time should be dedicated to question and answer sessions, troubleshooting, and discussions of the project.

Let's examine NaNoWriMo in further detail.

NaNoWriMo is:

- The acronym for **Na**tional **No**vel **Wri**ting **Mo**nth, which is officially in November of each year.

- Free—there is no charge for you or your students to use NaNoWriMo.

- An opportunity like no other—writers from all over the world mentally prepare for this and come together in a bonding opportunity to support one another's writing endeavors.

This has become so popular in recent years that there is now a dedicated section of NaNoWriMo for teachers to utilize in the classroom. This helps ensure safety measures are being followed and prevents adults from gaining access to the students. Teachers are able to use this to encourage students to brainstorm in their creative writing process, write, rewrite, critique, and ultimately publish. Although it is covered in greater detail in the publishing chapter, it is worth noting that CreateSpace.com, an online publishing source, provides all writers whom meet their word goals five copies of their completed work free of charge. This is a fabulous motivator for the students!

EVALUATIONS/ASSESSMENTS

The grading rubric for this assignment demonstrates great diversity. This assignment naturally forms a cohort of students working toward a similar goal with coordinating aspirations. There should be discussion to both support and encourage the students. While person to person peer discussion is a strength within the classroom, a blog for sharing information will boost that communication and means of cheerleading one another along.

Upon completion of the initial assignment on November 30, the following month of December (typically a short school month due to holiday breaks) is ideal for revising and editing the work. This is when the writer should return to the narrative and fine-tune the initial product.

The rubric focuses on the nuts and bolts of the actual novel, not on the educator's personal appreciation of the story itself. It is imperative to grade based on the student meeting the criteria rather than on your personal enjoyment of the story.

Before the First Lesson Plan

Take some time to familiarize yourself with NaNoWriMo. Sign up for your own account and walk yourself through the process. It would be both encouraging and enlightening to sign up to write your own novel with the students.

If you choose to pursue this in November utilizing the NaNoWriMo site and tools, you should have ample time to get a feel for your students and of their capabilities to accurately guide them in setting individual goals.

BASIC LESSON PLAN

Day 1—Number the steps so they become faster reference talking points

- Introduce project.
- Brainstorm writing ideas with the class.
- Hand out glossary of terms to study. While some terms may seem elementary, many students use words daily without ever learning the actual definition. It is critical that they understand the meanings to fulfill the expectations.
- Set word goals.
- Set a deadline for the project.
- Give basic guidelines to students (where to blog, how often to blog, expected outcome of project).

Daily throughout length of project—

- Reminders of meeting word count goals and blog entry goals
- Touch base with students struggling to meet goals
- Review posts and responds if necessary in blog
- Answer questions

In the final days—

- Follow-up with students to ensure word counts are being met
- Test students on vocabulary terms

Deadline Day—

- Students turn in initial draft with final word count.
- Introduce the next step (see "Publishing" chapter).

Novel-Writing Lesson Plan Breakdown

In-Class Discussion and Support with Writing as Homework

Overview

In the initial classroom discussion, it may be necessary to provide some ideas to the students for writing. It is a daunting task to be told to simply "write a novel" of so many words. One way to kick this off is to have a brainstorming session with the class. There are several methods to use: 1) listing favorite movies/songs/television shows/sports/people; 2) listing various eras (Depression/Gangster/Victorian/a particular decade); 3) listing favorite activities (sports/games/vacations). Once you begin listing, students begin to think on their own topics in which they are personally interested.

By the end of the discussion, each student should have at a minimum a topic or character or location on which to base their novel. With that said, it is imperative to clarify to the students that any of this may change once they begin the writing process. The goal is to get them to write, write, write! This is an assignment which may be used at 6–12 grade level, and the only customization necessary is that of the individual word count. It is very open and liberating, giving the students creative license to create their own assignment. In doing so, the motivation level should elevate and the passion for the assignment should be obvious. There are some guidelines you may want to include to assist the students in getting started, such as a blueprint for a novel.

This discussion should occur approximately one week prior to the start date. You will want to introduce the ideas, set the word count, and have the students register with the NaNoWriMo site in advance in order to not lose valuable writing time. Thirty days goes by VERY quickly!

Because this is a lengthy project, it would be wise to encourage the student to not only save the work to a computer and/or flash drive, but to also email a copy of the work to him/herself each day just in case the computer crashes, the flash drive is lost, or any other unforeseen and painful loss occurs. It would be awful for a student to, on day 28, lose his/her computer and have no record of his/her hard work. Consider these novel development guidelines:

INTRODUCTION

1. Use a fabulous opening line to draw the reader in. Hook the reader from the start.

2. Introduce main characters. Reveal key traits, the good, the bad, and the ugly. Make sure the reader knows your characters. Consider a discussion on the role of the protagonist, antagonist, round, and flat characters.

3. Create the setting, tone, and theme of story. Where is this taking place? At what time in history (or the future)?

BODY

1. Build from the introduction, creating more detail for the characters and setting, and introduce new characters.

2. Introduce the conflict. Nearly every novel has a conflict/problem/tragedy of some sort. If the student did not introduce it with the hook at the beginning of the story, it needs to be introduced now and built upon. Give great detail, and build the story as you would a house—from the ground up with a solid foundation and great support surrounding it.

3. Use vivid language to develop all aspects of the story. Use vernacular appropriate to the time/place/location/character.

CONCLUSION

1. Clearly demonstrate the resolution of the conflict, theme or plot.

2. Or, if you prefer to leave an open ending for a future volume keep the reader in suspense.

You may choose to pick some of your favorite lines from novels to share with the class to demonstrate clever hooks, vivid language, and plot development. Students should be encouraged to reflect on their own favorite novels, novelists, or writing styles to determine what it is about those works that speak to them.

Discussing NaNoWriMo—Time 30 minutes

After you have engaged your students with the novel assignment parameters, you will want to discuss the premise of NaNoWriMo, set word counts, and present the expectations of this assignment.

First, the students will have to set the word count goal. You then need to explain that they have 30 days in which to complete this—no exceptions. Daily word count updates are encouraged, and you should set a mandatory update (every three days, every five days, or whatever you see fit). No student should neglect this. It needs to be clear that the novel will be turned in, and word count will factor into the grade.

Secondly, the students will be required to work together and post on the blog with the other students in addition to discussing and contributing in class. On the blog, students will be expected to ask questions, answer questions of others, encourage one another, discuss ideas (trouble spots, frustrations, etc.), and offer support. Novels are not group projects, however, and they should be working individually on their own novels. Sharing ideas is a great tool, though. In the classroom, students should ask questions, share concerns, and discuss the project as a group. It is imperative that students participate in both online blogging and in-class discussions.

Finally, you'll explain a few words about the critique process. Students must know that all feedback in NaNoWriMo must be constructive, not destructive. The students are to examine the merits of the work, not whether or not they personally like the work. Negativity will not be tolerated, and that must be made clear.

In Class Writing—Optional

If you are lucky enough to have access to computers or iPads in the classroom for each student, you may opt to have in-class writing time 3–5 times in the 30 day writing process. If you do not have enough for each student but you have access to a few iPads or computers, you may want to offer writing time at lunch or before/after school for students requiring assistance.

Final Word Count

The only time the student is required to upload the work to the NaNoWriMo site is on the final day. NaNoWriMo verifies the word count. There is often some discrepancy, so the student may want to upload it to the official site prior to the due date to verify the word counts match. After the word count is validated, NaNoWriMo deletes the work. The work will not be "stolen" by another writer.

Collaboration Day—Day 31

This should be a day of grandiose celebration! Your students have just accomplished a huge goal, and it should be treated as such. It would be really fun to have a "debriefing day" with a pizza party (afternoon) or bagels (breakfast), discussing the likes and dislikes of this project, how it could be made better, and what was learned throughout this process. Some students may even wish to share excerpts from their work with the class.

However, it is not over. Days 1–30 were simply the prewriting, the building of the house, as explained earlier. Now the walls need to be painted, the carpet needs to be laid, and the decorations need to be hung.

As mentioned earlier, December is a short month due to the holiday breaks. This is a good time to work on revisions and cleaning up the novel. Students may wish to partner up at this point to read one another's work and offer suggestions and make corrections. Teamwork should be encouraged at this time as collaboration is vital in the writing process.

The new goal is now set: to clean up the work to meet the standard of publication. If you set the completion date as the first of the year, the students have one month to make the improvements. At that point, the students will be able to submit it to <u>CreateSpace.com</u>, receive their five copies, and you can hold a publishing party (see "Publishing" chapter for details).

Creating a NanoWriMo Account

1. Point your browser to <u>ywp.nanowrimo.org.</u>

2. On the home page you should see a link to "Sign Up" in the upper right hand corner.

3. Create your account.

Since NaNoWriMo is only available during November one can set up a private class Facebook group as an alternative to be used anytime throughout the year. Please see Facebook Class Fictional Writing Caper lesson for private group set up instructions.

NaNoWriMo Rubric

Student Name

Writing Variable	1-4 Needs Work	5-6 Fair Job	7-8 Good Job	9-10 Terrific	Score	Common Core Strand for Secondary Educators
Setting	It is unclear and/or confusing as to the time and place of the story	The setting is vague and in the process of being developed	The reader understands either the time or place of the story, but the setting is not entirely clear	It is clear where and when the writing is taking place. There is no doubt in the reader's mind		W.9-12.3 W.9-12.4
Character Development	Characters are not developed; minimum effort made	Characters have some personality, but more variety is needed, more characters are needed, stronger descriptions are required	Characters are developed, but there is something lacking in the connection with reader; needs more development	Demonstrates a variety of characters (protagonist, antagonist, flat, round), has strong description of each, reader feels he/she knows the characters		W.9-12.3 W.9-12.4
Plot	Lacking plot	Some development of plot evident	Decent grasp of plot development; needs some fine tuning	Excellent development of plot; reader is able to easily follow		W.9-12.3 W.9-12.4
Sequence	Out of order	Some development of plot evident	Story is in order	Easy to follow, good sequencing		W.9-12.3 W.9-12.4
Creativity/ Originality	Not much effort put in	Decent idea, needs more creative elements	Includes a variety of creative elements and original ideas	Strong effort made in making this original; creative aspects are strong		W.9-12.4
Details	Minimal details offered.	Details in developmental stage.	Details are good, the reader has a feel for the setting, plot, characters	Details are vivid, strong, and embrace the reader. A picture is continuously painted in the mind of the reader		W.9-12.3

NaNoWriMo Rubric

Criterion					Standards
Dialogue	The reader feels as if he/she is part of the conversation. The dialogue pulls the reader into the conversation	Characters have strong dialogue	Conversation is developing	Very little dialogue	W.9-12.3
Vocabulary*	Highly effective in using a variety of words.	Vocabulary is at grade level; good use of variety of words and expressions.	Some development of word variance evident.	Very limited range of word use.	W.9-12.3 W.9-12.4
Grammar*	There are no serious grammar errors.	There are fewer than 10 serious grammar errors.	There are fewer than 15 serious grammar errors.	There are 15 or more serious grammar errors.	W.9-12.3 W.9-12.4
Mechanics/ Spelling*	All sentences use correct spelling, capitalization, punctuation, and end marks.	There are fewer than 10 errors in spelling, capitalization, punctuation, and end marks.	There are fewer than 15 errors in spelling, capitalization, punctuation, and end marks.	There are 15 or more errors in spelling, capitalization, punctuation, and end marks.	W.9-12.4 W.9-12.4
Blog Initial	Exceeded the blog entry requirement; quality of feedback is strong.	Met the blog entry requirement; quality of feedback is decent.	Met 75% of the blog entry requirement; moderate quality of feedback.	Met 50% or less of blog entry requirement; low quality of feedback.	W.9-12.6 W.9-12.10
Cohort Peer Support	Offered extra support to those peers in need .	Worked well with others; demonstrated support of peer.	Made a minimal effort with peer support..	Did not make an appropriate effort with peers	W.9-12.6 W.9-12.10
Word Count Goal	Exceeded goal	Met goal	Met 75% of the word count goal	Met 50% or less of word count goal	W.9-12.10
	Average for Best Score Out of 10				

*Do not neglect to take into account a student may use slang in his/her novel and this should not be marked down if used correctly.

CREATESPACE FOR YOUR CLASS

"There are three difficulties in authorship: to write anything worth publishing, to find honest men to publish it, and to find sensible men to read it." ~ Charles Caleb Colton. Truer words were never spoken. The greatest accomplishment in a writer's life is being published. It is the goal for which every writer strives, as it brings a sense of success and allows the author to share his/her writings with anyone willing to read the work.

Publishing tends to be a misunderstood word, especially to students. While the popular definition of publishing involves the distribution of books via bookstores, publishing is simply the duplicating of a work for distribution, from the days of handwriting copies to printing presses to copy machines. Today, with technology, it includes the use of computers, social media, and classrooms. Publication no longer requires a bound book, but instead, any work on display for the visual entertainment of others, even if it is hanging on the front of a refrigerator with a magnet! On the flip side, the publication is not required to even be tangible; eBooks are gaining popularity due to the growing selection of ereaders.

OPTIONS

As an educator, you have many options in how to pursue the publication aspect of the common core. First, you must identify which option will be most effective with the assignment you have given. As stated in the NaNoWriMo chapter, any student completing the 30 day challenge of writing a novel is able to publish, free of charge, 10 copies of his or her book through CreateSpace. This is a fabulous opportunity! It is recommended that one copy be provided to the classroom to build a library for the teacher. This will assist other students in the future as they are able to see first-hand the potential fruits of their labor. It is a great motivator for these young authors.

There are other self-publishing options out there. Lulu.com is another to create and print your own book online. Lulu.com allows the writer to utilize any format and print only what he or she needs. If you prefer, you may also choose to take the ebook route and allow students to upload their books to Kindle (Amazon) or Nook (Barnes and Noble). Should you choose this, though, it is still recommended to have a hard copy of the book available for the party and to keep on hand for classroom reference in the future. This would also make an outstanding display for the open house the following year to show parents and students what to expect in this class.

EVALUATIONS/ASSESSMENTS

The grading rubric for this assignment will focus on the publication and distribution of the work. It is straight-forward.

Before the First Lesson Plan

Examine the publishing sites to see what will work best for your class. If you engage in the NaNoWriMo, CreateSpace is ideal because it offers a free opportunity to your students. If you choose to take another route for your writing assignment, please examine the other publishing options discussed.

BASIC LESSON PLAN

Day 1—

- Introduce project.

- Hand out glossary of terms to study. While some

terms may seem elementary, many students use words daily without ever learning the actual definition. It is critical that they understand the meanings to fulfill the expectations.

- Set a deadline for the project. A deadline is simply the day all students must have their work submitted to the publisher.

- Explain how to set up an author page on <u>Amazon.com</u> and assign that to each student.

Deadline Day—

- Students confirm that the work has been submitted.

- Class will discuss the process and how they feel about this project.

Distribution Day/Publishing Party

This is where the publishing hits the really fun climax. When the hard copies of the books have arrived, the assignment is nearly complete. Keep in mind that if you are unable to go through a publisher, another option would be to print off one or two copies of each book and spiral bind it at the school. While a "professional" book would be fabulous, any copy of the book will work to complete this project and meet the standard.

At this point, you will sit with the class, create invitations to the parents and staff, and invite them to a publishing party. Ideally, you will use a large open space in the school to set this up. The students will create displays and show off their completed works in a book fair fashion. It is similar to a book signing whereas the students will be on hand to discuss and promote their books and answer questions. Have punch and cookies. Make this one big party demonstrating the success of your class.

Don't forget to invite the media in to cover this. The students are stars—promote them! Finally, have each student donate one or two copies of the book to a silent auction. Allow the guests to bid on the books. How you use the money you raise should be up to the class. You could donate it toward a scholarship, give it to a charity (ideally one working to improve literacy) chosen by the students, or use it for library improvements. You have a fabulous opportunity to do so much with a simply assignment; make the most of it.

CREATESPACE RUBRIC						
Student Name						
	1-4 Needs Work	5-6 Fair Job	7-8 Good Job	9-10 Terrific	Score	Common Core Strand for Secondary Educators
Student's work is acceptable for publication	Writing unclear, not to task	Writing is a work in progress; needs direction	Clear, coherent writing; well-developed	Exceeded all expectations		W.9-12.4
Student developed and strengthened writing per the assignment	Not well-developed	Some revising and editing evident	Well-planned, revised, edited, and rewritten	Excelled at the revision process and created an excellent writing project		W.9-12.5
Published Work	Did not meet the guidelines for publishing	Published with at least one source (hard copy)	Published using the Internet as well as hard copy	Marketed work, participated in publishing party, used the Internet for publishing, created a hard copy		W.9-12.6

Appendix A:
Advanced YouTube Video Editing

For more advanced technology driven students, they may download supporting YouTube videos of their choice and edit particular segments with proper video citation (rolling credits at the end of their response) and post their complete response video package without the YouTube annotation hyperlinks. These students can use the free software mentioned earlier. They will need to download and install on their own computer or one available from your class/school.

Enter your ELA class. In consideration of the YouTube Controversial Video Summary & Rebuttal students can download several videos, decide which scenes (frames along a timeline) are controversial, and include these scenes in a new broader montage video. This new video can serve as an argumentative thesis, claim, or defense or to enhance the background (historical perspective) or investigative nature of another controversial issue under class analysis. This new video can provide a creative class outlet and also may be beneficial when just simply providing a YouTube hyperlink to several videos is too cumbersome and cannot enable various viewpoints to be displayed in one simple viewing.

Bear in mind that one cannot simply right click on a YouTube video and download it. While one can upload a video prepared using a variety of file formats such as: .MOV, .MPEG4, .AVI, .WMV and several others tinyurl. com/lvxo79k YouTube converts the file to Adobe Flash or HTML5. There are various reasons for converting millions of videos including the speed of which videos are viewed online, their resolution up to 1080i, the ability for smart-phone browsers to view, computer chip speeds, and for Google YouTube servers to operate efficiently.

Another reason YouTube converts the videos is to slow the rate of piracy. However, like authors who para-phrase and quote various articles for various publication purposes—video frames, scenes, and pieces, can be used in other videos when fair use, educational purposes, and not for profit means are applied appropriately.

Numerous articles abound all over the Internet on how to convert YouTube videos and there are a variety of free You-Tube conversation software packages one can install. Perhaps the only catch, if you will, when it comes to such free software, is their tendency to include adware or other bloatware.

One can download such a program and can then typi-cally remove the bloatware or add on browser tool bars later. CNet is typically a reliable reviewer of such freeware and has recommended YTD Video Downloader. This par-ticular converter downloads a YouTube file and coverts it to MPEG4. tinyurl.com/6segcwz. YTD also is available as a paid version which offers more options.

All of these conversion programs are fairly easy to use. One simply copies and pastes the YouTube video web address (URL) into the software where indicated, click a start button, and the download begins.

Basically, the program and similar ones like it ask the user to copy and paste the video's YouTube URL (Univer-sal Resource Locator), the web address, into a particular area of the software program.

The program retrieves and converts the YouTube video into an MPEG or other useful editing format that will be stored on the computer. Using any available video edit-ing software program, the student can intersperse relative defending video clips in between his or her rebuttal response along the video editing timeline window. Follow the guidelines the same as in Lesson II: Controversial Issue Summary and Rebuttal but with the newly edited video(s).

For general YouTube video editing tips visit <u>youtube.com/t/creators corner</u>.

Appendix B: YouTube Permission Slip

Friday, November 2, 2015

Dear Student Participant:

We take pride on innovative educational opportunities for students to learn in a variety of different ways. Recently several institutions have begun to incorporate lesson plans using social media since the venue is enjoyed by so many students and faculty alike. Based on this popular learning format we would like your permission to post YouTube videos you create to our English class YouTube channel located at _____ < List URL here.

You agree that your cooperation is done so royalty free now or in the future. Your work will be displayed permanently at this channel URL: _____. You may opt out by doing a standard traditional essay or another assignment offered by your instructor.

Only the instructor, yourself, and other students in the class will participate in the writing exercises through this YouTube channel. Your access is contingent upon your current Google or Google+ YouTube user name (identity) and email. If none exists your instructor can help you obtain one at accounts.google.com/SignUp. While no social media network is 100 percent safe, we have taken every precaution that the site not be marketed or promoted in the YouTube network. You are free to provide the channel web address and the instructor is free to provide the address to teachers or those interested in YouTube lesson plans.

Your signature below indicates you agree to these YouTube participation terms:

_____	_____	_____
Print Name	Sign Name	Date

Thank you for your cooperation and we look forward to a great learning experience!

Sincerely, _____ < Enter your name here

APPENDIX C:
GENERIC SOCIAL MEDIA PERMISSION SLIP

[School Logo/Letterhead]

Friday, November 2, 2015

To Whom It May Concern:

The _____ School District prides itself on innovative educational opportunities for students to learn in a variety of different ways. Recently several institutions have begun to incorporate lesson plans using social media since the venue is enjoyed by so many students and faculty alike. Based on this popular learning format we would like your permission to create a WordPress account on behalf of your child for use in writing exercises tied to the Common Core.

Only the instructor, your child, and other students in the class will participate in the writing exercises through WordPress. Only your child's first name or a pseudo name will appear in the discussions. While no social media network is 100 percent safe, we have taken every precaution to ensure only the faculty member and students will share in the learning exercises that will take place during class and occasionally in the evening for homework, if required.

Your signature will allow your child to immediately participate:

_____   _____   _____
Print Name   Sign Name   Date

Once your approval is received, your child will be furnished with a WordPress unique site name. Parents are encouraged to logon and to monitor the lessons by clicking the follow button and confirming via email. Please have your child return the signed slip as soon as possible to his or her English Language Arts instructor. Thank you for your cooperation and we look forward to a great new learning experience!

Sincerely,

THE ENGLISH LANGUAGE ARTS TEAM

APPENDIX D

FICTION WRITING RUBRIC

Student Name: _____

Writing Variable	1-4 Needs Work	5-6 Fair Job	7-8 Good Job	9-10 Terrific	Score	Common Core Strand for Secondary Educators
Setting	It is unclear and/or confusing as to the time and place of the story	The setting is vague and in the process of being developed	The reader understands either the time or place of the story, but the setting is not entirely clear	It is clear where and when the writing is taking place. There is no doubt in the reader's mind		W.9-12.3 W.9-12.4
Character Development	Characters are not developed; minimum effort made	Characters have some personality, but more variety is needed, more characters are needed, stronger descriptions are required	Characters are developed, but there is something lacking in the connection with reader; needs more development	Demonstrates a variety of characters (protagonist, antagonist, flat, round), has strong description of each, reader feels he/she knows the characters		W.9-12.3 W.9-12.4
Plot	Lacking plot	Some development of plot evident	Decent grasp of plot development; needs some fine tuning	Excellent development of plot; reader is able to easily follow		W.9-12.3 W.9-12.4
Sequence	Out of order	Some development of plot evident	Story is in order	Easy to follow, good sequencing		
Creativity/ Originality	Not much effort put in	Decent idea, needs more creative elements	Includes a variety of creative elements and original ideas	Strong effort made in making this original; creative aspects are strong		W.9-12.4
Details	Minimal details offered.	Details in developmental stage.	Details are good, the reader has a feel for the setting, plot, characters	Details are vivid, strong, and embrace the reader. A picture is continuously painted in the mind of the reader		W.9-12.3

APPENDIX D

Dialogue	Very little dialogue	Conversation is developing	Characters have strong dialogue	The reader feels as if he/she is part of the conversation. The dialogue pulls the reader into the conversation	W.9-12.3
Vocabulary*	Very limited range of word use.	Some development of word variance evident.	Vocabulary is at grade level; good use of variety of words and expressions.	Highly effective in using a variety of words.	W.9-12.3 W.9-12.4
Grammar*	There are 15 or more serious grammar errors.	There are fewer than 15 serious grammar errors.	There are fewer than 10 serious grammar errors.	There are no serious grammar errors.	W.9-12.3 W.9-12.4
Mechanics/ Spelling*	There are 15 or more errors in spelling, capitalization, punctuation, and end marks.	There are fewer than 15 errors in spelling, capitalization, punctuation, and end marks.	There are fewer than 10 errors in spelling, capitalization, punctuation, and end marks.	All sentences use correct spelling, capitalization, punctuation, and end marks.	W.9-12.4 W.9-12.4
Blog Initial Collaborative Entry	Met 50% or less of blog entry requirement; low quality of feedback.	Met 75% of the blog entry requirement; moderate quality of feedback.	Met the blog entry requirement; quality of feedback is decent.	Exceeded the blog entry requirement; quality of feedback is strong.	W.9-12.6 W.9-12.10
Cohort Peer Support	Did not make an appropriate effort with peers	Made a minimal effort with peer support.	Worked well with others; demonstrated support of peer.	Offered extra support to those peers in need .	W.9-12.6 W.9-12.10
Word Count Goal	Met 50% or less of word count goal	Met 75% of the word count goal	Met goal	Exceeded goal	W.9-12.10
				Average for Best Score Out of 10	

Do not neglect to take into account a student may use slang in his/her novel and this should not be marked down if used correctly.

Appendix E

Non-Fiction Writing & Collaboration Rubric

Student Name

Writing Variable	1-4 Needs Work	5-6 Fair Job	7-8 Good Job	9-10 Terrific	Score	Common Core Strand for Secondary Educators
Thesis	Thesis is not clear. Reads like an editorial.	Thesis mentioned with one variable, but not well-developed.	Thesis is clear and contains at least two variables.	Thesis has well-defined variables and expressed authoritatively.		W.9-12.1 W.9-12.2 W.6-8.1 / W.6-8.1a W.6-8.2 W.6-8.2a
Evidence	Points are confusing and not connected to main topic.	Average development of points presented.	Evidence is presented well; needs fine tuning.	Points are valid, plentiful, clear, and concise.		W.9-12.1 W.9-12.2 W.9-12.7 W.9-12.8 W.9-12.9 W.6-8.1 W.6-8.1b W.6-8.1c W.6-8.1d / W.6-8.2 W.6-8.2b W.6-8.2c W.6-8.2d W.6-8.2e W.6-8.7 W.6-8.8 W.6-8.9 W.6-8.9b
Argument	Not at all convincing.	Somewhat convincing; needs more support, facts, and evidence.	Convincing, but needs fine tuning.	Excellent presentation, very convincing, strong development of argument to support thesis.		W.9-12.1 W.9-12.2 W.6-8.1 W.6-8.1b W.6-8.1c W.6-8.1d / W.6-8.2 W.6-8.2b W.6-8.2c W.6-8.2d W.6-8.2e W.6-8.9b

APPENDIX E

	Level 1	Level 2	Level 3	Level 4	Standards	Standards
Details	Minimal details offered.	Details in developmental stage.	Details are good; the reader has a feel for the stance the writer has taken.	Details are vivid, strong, and embrace the reader; the argument is convincing based on the details supporting it.	W.9-12.1 W.9-12.2 W.6-8.1 W.6-8.1b W.6-8.1c W.6-8.1d	W.6-8.2 W.6-8.2b W.6-8.2c W.6-8.2d W.6-8.2e
Conclusion	Conclusion Summary not clear and concise; introduces new information; does not reiterate thesis.	Summary in development stage; needs work.	Decent summary, but could be stronger.	Summarizes, does not introduce new information, reiterates thesis.	W.9-12.1 W.9-12.2 W.6-8.1 W.6-8.1c W.6-8.1d	W.6-8.1e W.6-8.2 W.6-8.2d W.6-8.2e W.6-8.2f
Vocabulary	Very limited range of word use; utilizes slang and/or attacks.	Some development of word variance evident; slang and/or attacks evident.	Vocabulary is at grade level; good use of variety of words and expressions.	Highly effective in using a variety of words; avoids attacks, slang, etc.	W.9-12.1 W.9-12.2 W.6-8.1 W.6-8.1a W.6-8.1c W.6-8.1d	W.6-8.1e W.6-8.2 W.6-8.2b W.6-8.2c W.6-8.2d W.6-8.2e
Grammar	There are 15 or more serious grammar errors.	There are fewer than 15 serious grammar errors.	There are fewer than 10 serious grammar errors.	There are no serious grammar errors.	W.9-12.1 W.9-12.2 W.6-8.1 W.6-8.1a W.6-8.1c W.6-8.1d	W.6-8.1e W.6-8.2 W.6-8.2b W.6-8.2c W.6-8.2d W.6-8.2e

Appendix E

Mechanics/ Spelling*	There are 15 or more errors in spelling, capitalization, punctuation, and end marks.	There are fewer than 15 errors in spelling, capitalization, punctuation, and end marks.	There are fewer than 10 errors in spelling, capitalization, punctuation, and end marks.	All sentences use correct spelling, capitalization, punctuation, and end marks.	W.9-12.1 W.9-12.2 W.6-8.1 W.6-8.1c W.6-8.1d	W.6-8.2 W.6-8.2c W.6-8.2d W.6-8.2e
Blog Initial Collaborative Entry	Not much effort	Decent idea, needs more creative elements such as figurative language	Includes a variety of creative elements and original ideas as figurative language	Strong effort made in making this original; creative aspects are strong as figurativelanguage	W.9-12.1 W.9-12.2 W.9-12.4-6 W.6-8.4	W.6-8.5 W.6-8.6 W.6-8.10
Cohort Peer Support	Did not make an appropriate effort with peers in class or electronically.	Made a minimal effort with peer support in class or electronically.	Worked well with others; demonstrated support of peers in class or electronically.	Offered extra support to those peers in need in class or electronically.	W.9-12.1 W.9-12.2 W.9-12.4-6	W.9-12.10 W.6-8.4 W.6-8.5
				Average for Best Score Out of 10		

Appendix F:
Adapting WordPress Blog Lessons to Blogger

As mentioned in the introduction, our initial book *Word-Press for Student Writing Projects* published by Brigantine Media/Compass Division features complete blogging lessons on essay, thesis writing, and quality source analysis. If you've purchased that book and want to adapt those lessons to Blogger, the instructions to follow can help you get started.

The following is a sample at readsumrespond.blogspot.com of a recent live Blogger classroom site designed for a newspaper article summary and response collaborative exercise. The flexibility behind the Blogger dashboard will allow you to keep the site unpublished from search engines as well as enable a host of permissions to allow either students to post with a Google+ account or simply open it up during the collaborative process to allow all access publicly.

Note that the navigation includes tabs that run horizontally along the header of the site. While you can create any number of pages in Blogger, in order to apply a menu tab like this, one must navigate inside the dashboard to "layout" and apply navigation in the form of a page menu app otherwise the student pages where their drafts can be posted separately will not readily show. Also keep in mind that these student menu tab pages do not show in most smartphones. Otherwise, Blogger has many apps that you can tie to the blog to track the most popular drafts and latest comments.

Google's Blogger is another tool in the king of social media's arsenal allowing users to reach exponentially expansive audiences. The free and versatile service is a complement to one's Google+ account, thus making it a smart blogging choice. And since the introduction of Google+, Google has made it clear that it will prominently list its own users higher in the Google search engine results compared to non-users (Bean 2013a; 2013b; 2013c; 2013d). While that notoriety may not be what your class-room seeks: your school may have an upcoming mandate or is currently using Google apps. The convenience having so many Google products in one place is attractive.

Initializing a Blogger Account

1. The process to get your Blogger site up and run-ning starts while being logged into your Gmail or Google+ account.

2. In your browser's address line, type in blogger.com.

3. Click on New Blog in the upper left page portion.

4. A new pop up window will appear. Here you can assign a blog title, web address that ends in .blogspot.com (Google will automatically check name availability), and any number of templates to make your blog unique.

5. Consider selecting a name that represents your class. You can use this one specifically for that purpose but you will not give up your ability to create other blogs.

6. Click the Create button. In about a minute your new blog will appear in your Blogger account.

7. You can create as many types of blogs as you wish and manage them at Blogger.com since the page will be permanently tied to your Google+ account.

8. To see your new empty blog with the template you selected, click or touch the View blog button. A separate window will launch. You can then toggle

from your <u>BlogSpot.com</u> page back to your Blogger home page. The <u>Blogger.com</u> home page is just a landing page that is not visible to the public. To post your first blog just click or touch the pencil icon.

9. You can build your page via a Google Docs word processing interface in text or HTML.

10. If you wish to add more pages from the <u>Blogger.com</u> home page click or touch the document icon. You can then add commenting features, track page statistics, add more individual page templates and a host of gadgets that can track popular pages and comments, great for a classroom collaboration writing lesson.

11. Please feel free to let us know your adaptation experience? Perhaps we can share it in a future book edition.

References

Adobe Systems, Incorporated. 2014. "Abode Premiere Elements 12/tech Specs."adobe.com/products/ premiere-elements/tech-specs.html.

Academy of American Poets. 2013a. "Poetic Forms &Techniques." poets.org/poetsorg/text/poetic-forms-techniques.

Academy of American Poets. 2013b. "Poetic form: Limerick." poets.org/poetsorg/text/poetic-form-limerick.

Angelou, M. 2014. "Maya AngelowGlobelRenaissance Woman." mayaangelou.com.

Barbeau, M. 2010. "Teaching writing with YouTube." Lore,Spring, 1-10.

Bean, E. 2013a. "Detroiters rev up your SEO: Join Google+ now." examiner.com/article/detroiters-rev-up-your-seo-join-google-now.

Bean, E. 2013b. "Freshly Squeezed Student Perspectives YouTube Channel." youtube.com/ channel/UCKdBvyA8Pr17rU9wxWsTUkg.

Bean, E. 2013c. "Freshly Squeezed Student Perspective YouTube Unpublished Channel." youtube.com/watch ?v=UXrY9Q9hemY&list=PLNvZCbSMBrGs18UtZYc vSsGAzfrfwqxdG.

Bean, E. 2013d. "Unenabling the Dangers of Smartphone Camera GPS Coordinates." examiner. com/article/tech-tip-now-unenabling-the-danger-of-smartphone-camera-gps-coordinates.

Bean, E. 2014a. "How to Create WordPress Student Blogs Aligned with Common Core writing standards," *Presented at the 2014 Society of Information Technology and Teacher Education 25th Annual Conference* (March 20, 2014). Jacksonville, FL: SITE.

Bean, E. 2014b. "YouTube for Common Core writing."
Presented at the *2014 7ᵗʰ International SLOAN-C
Symposium: Emerging Technologies for Online
Learning*, Dallas, TX, April 10, 2014.

Bean, E., and E. Waszak. 2013. "YouTube for Common
Core writing." Presented at the *2ⁿᵈAnnual Michigan
Google Educator's Conference*, Brighton High School,
Brighton, MI, Nov. 6, 2013.

Bean, E., and E. Waszak. 2014. WordPress for Student
Writing Projects. St. Johnsbury, VT: Brigantine Media:
Compass Division, SocialMediaLessonPlans.com.

Famous Poets and Poems. 2006. "Famous Poets and
Poems, A to Z." famouspoetsandpoems.com/poets.html.

Google. 2014a. "Create_channel." youtube.com/create_channel.

Google. 2014b. "Educate, Engage, and Inspire your
Students with Video!.." youtube.com/schools.

Google. 2014c. "Up Up and Away – Long Videos for More
Users." youtube-global.blogspot.com/2010/12/up-up-and-
away-long-videos-for-more.html.

Google. 2014d. "YouTube Community Guidelines."
youtube.com/t/community_guidelines.

Griffin, M. 1982. "Maya Angelou Interview
(Merv Griffin Show 1982)." youtube.com/
watch?v=pFSjC6D5j5U.

Long River Review. 2010. "A Brief History of Poetry
Reading." longriverreview.com/blog/2010/a-brief-
history-of-poetry-readings.

Mayora, C. 2010. "Using YouTube to Encourage
Authentic Writing in EFL Classrooms." *TESL
Reporter* 42(1): 1-12.

Mehrabian, A. 2007. *Nonverbal communications*. New
Brunswick, NJ: Aldine Transcation.

Mullen, L. 2011. "How to Persuade-With Ethos, Pathos, or Logos?" chronicle.com/blogs/profhacker/how-to-persuade-with-ethos-pathos-or-logos/35431.

Page, J. 2012. "Interview with Maya Angelou." youtube.com/watch?v=hSY7PokqMXk.

Strate, L. 2004. "A Media Ecology Review." *Communication Research Trends* 23 (2)., 3-48.

Wideen, K. 2104. "Using Social Media as a Teaching Tool." mrswideen.com/2014/05/using-social-media-as-teaching-tool.html?spref=tw.

Glossary of Related Popular Social Media Terms

YouTube

Annotation—A feature that allows the incorporation of a hyperlink overlaid in the video at any point.

Dislike—A public poll expressing the number of visitors who chose to dislike the video. It is not a scientific poll.

Like—A public poll expressing the number of visitors who chose to like a video. It is not a scientific poll.

Channel—A YouTube site with a specific theme like one for your classroom.

Hit—The total number of views accrued by a video.

Playlist—A method to combine videos under one category so when one is viewed the remaining videos will automatically load in sequential order and are visible together.

Subscription—A button that allows visitors to follow your channel. If you post a new video, they will receive an update.

Thumbs Down—A poll available next to a comment that allows visitors to vote down a comment so it appears physically lower or less prominent.

Thumbs Up—A poll available next to a comment that allows visitors to vote up a comment so it appears physically higher and more prominent.

Unpublished Link—A Video or playlist of videos that cannot be indexed in Google nor are available through searching YouTube.

Viral—A video that has received so many hits that its popularity has become ubiquitous throughout YouTube and in many other websites and mediums.

Facebook

Comment—To share a thought on someone else's status update or to respond to a comment made on one's own post.

Group—A facebook channel that can be private for a variety of communication purposes including a unpublished class forum.

Like—A public poll expressing the number of visitors who have read the post.

Share—The ability to repost on your own page an item viewed on another page.

Status Update—A post that lets your friends or group know what's on your mind.

NaNoWriMo

NaNoWriMo—Abbreviation for National Novel Writing Month, which runs November 1–November 30 of each year.

Admin or Administrator—An authorized worker posting on or maintaining the website.

Bump—This is when a person replies to a post merely to send it back to the top of the forum listing.

Flame—Also known as a "Troll." This person instigates by attacking a post, person, or opinion or generally abuses another. It is most often a personal attack, and flamers/trolls often find great satisfaction in receiving responses from people with their posts. Responding to a flame/troll is not usually advisable. Trolls actively seek out controversial topics and join the conversation for the sake of argument. If you believe that someone is committing this abuse, please report his/her post(s) to the moderator.

Flamebait—A post that is designed to generate a flame. Topics are posted to lure in trolls and begin controversy. Tread lightly, and be careful with whom you choose to engage.

Forum—A forum is an area on the site where the topics are divided into various areas of interest. These topics are set up to be advantageous to the user to make it easier to find others with common interests.

Lurker—A site user who reads what others have to say but doesn't post.

Moderator or Mod—A host for a forum. The moderator is there to help by answering any questions and to settle disputes on the site. On the NaNoWriMo forums, moderator names are in red at the top of the forum page and on the forum list next to the title of the forum lounge.

NaNovel—A novel created during National Novel Writing Month.

NaNovelist—The author of a novel completed during NaNoWriMo.

Newbie—A person new to the forum, also called a n00b.

NSFW—Not Safe For Work—A caution very important to teachers and students. This warning indicates that the links lead to inappropriate text or images not acceptable to be viewed at work or by minors.

Post—A post is any single item placed in the forum by a person. A post may be an original post to spark discussion, or it may be a response to an existing post.

Thread—A conversation on a forum is called a "thread" or "topic." The original author posts the initial thread, and others respond to that post or to subsequent posts in the thread. It should stay on topic, but if an interesting conversation develops, a poster may prefer to break off and for another post regarding the new topic The abbreviation OP is used to refer to the "original poster," or the person who started the topic.

Topic—Any threaded conversation on the forums started by a post—see above.

Troll—A troll is a person whose sole goal on a forum is to antagonize others and inspire them to respond. Most of the time it's harmless. This can escalate to Flames, or people inciting anger. Some people enjoy engaging with trolls, but typically, nothing positive comes from joining in these posts.

WiFi—Wireless internet access, found at many coffee houses, libraries, bookstores, and other public places.

Wrimo—A writer who participates in National Novel Writing Month.

FICTIONAL TERMS

Antagonist—The principal character in opposition with the main character.

Character—The person or persons depicted in a story, narrative, or drama.

Conclusion—The ending of a story.

Cohort—A group of people working together on a common project with a common goal.

Dialogue—A conversation between two or more people, often times between characters in a book, play, or movie.

Description—A statement in which the person describing paints a picture in the mind of the receiver by incorporating colorful language and vivid examples.

First Person—Writing a story utilizing the pronouns "I" or "we."

Flat Character—An uncomplicated character; he/she does not impact the story.

Narrative—A story presented as a spoken or written account of connected events.

Pacing—The rate of movement from one point, section, or element in literature to another.

Plot—The storyline; how the story's sequence of events occurs. The plot should develop into a beginning, middle, and end.

Protagonist—The leading or main character in a story.

Reflection—Interpretation and opinion of a story, followed by comparison to other literature or comparable events in life.

Round Character—A complex character; one who may undergo great changes within the story.

Second Person—Writing a story utilizing the pronoun "you."

Sensory Language—Utilizing the five senses when selecting descriptive words in writing to create vivid images for the reader.

Setting—The scene (also known as Mise en Scene) in which the story is taking place.

Sequence—The continuous order in which events occur.

Time Management—Analyzing and prioritizing events in order to most effectively utilize time available to accomplish the goals at hand.

Third Person—The narrator is not actively participating in the story. There are three types of third person point of view.

Third Person Limited—This is the same as omniscient with the exception the narrator only knows the thoughts and emotions of one, sometimes two, characters. The narrator is limited in his or her knowledge.

Third Person Objective—The narrator is a detached observer. He/She is unaware of the characters' thoughts or emotions. He/She can only report what is said and done. This is akin to an audience member attending a play or movie. The person is only privy to what is seen; he/she has no insight as to the thoughts of the actor. Omniscient You are everywhere at once.

Third Person Omniscient—uses pronouns such as he, she, it, or the name of the character. The narrator, an outsider looking in, knows all, sees all, and reports all. The narrator is aware of the thoughts and emotions of all characters.

About the Authors

Erik Bean, Ed.D. is interim dean of the CXR Institute and a fellow at the Center for Leadership Studies and Educational Research (CLSER) where he studies student customer experience (CX) in order to effectively engage them. He holds a doctorate in education from University of Phoenix School of Advanced Studies and has served as a department chair, university professor, curriculum developer, online instructor, and has taught composition for more than 15 years. Erik's first Westphalia book, ***Rigorous Grading Using Microsoft Word: Plus Google Docs*** (September 2014) allows teachers to save time grading while providing detailed feedback.

Emily Waszak is an accomplished creative writing and English composition teacher and author of self-help and children's books. Her latest 2015 book, ***Duck Eggs*** is one of three new children's stories due out in 2015. Emily Waszak has worked in a variety of communication arenas. She also is a motivational speaker and has conducted writing workshops for middle and high school students in the suburban Detroit, Michigan area where she resides.

For more tips and news about Erik and Emily's social media lesson plans and to purchase other books, please visit: SocialMediaLessonPlans.com or GradingEfficiently.com.

Printed in Great Britain
by Amazon.co.uk, Ltd.,
Marston Gate.